Fashion and Class

Fashion and Class

Rachel Worth

BLOOMSBURY VISUAL ARTS
LONDON • NEW YORK • OXFORD • NEW DELHI • SYDNEY

BLOOMSBURY VISUAL ARTS
Bloomsbury Publishing Plc
50 Bedford Square, London, WC1B 3DP, UK
1385 Broadway, New York, NY 10018, USA

BLOOMSBURY, BLOOMSBURY VISUAL ARTS and the Diana logo are trademarks of
Bloomsbury Publishing Plc

First published in Great Britain 2020

For legal purposes the Acknowledgements on p. x constitute an extension
of this copyright page.

Cover design: Sharon Mah
Cover image: Interior of Litton Mill, Derbyshire, UK, 1933.
(© Hulton Archive/Getty Images)

A catalogue record for this book is available from the British Library.

A catalog record for this book is available from the Library of Congress.

ISBN: HB: 978-1-8478-8816-7
PB: 978-1-8478-8815-0
ePDF: 978-0-8578-5495-7
eBook: 978-0-8578-5494-0

Typeset by Newgen KnowledgeWorks Pvt. Ltd., Chennai, India
Printed and bound in Great Britain

To find out more about our authors and books visit www.bloomsbury.com
and sign up for our newsletters.

Contents

Illustrations

Acknowledgements

My love for social history emerged when I was at secondary school, and grew in large part because of the knowledge and infectious enthusiasm of an inspirational history teacher, Ruth Newman, who encouraged me to study the subject at university. She also introduced me to original historical research through E. P. Thompson's pioneering *The Making of the English Working Class* (1963), a book to which I always return when I want to be reminded of why history is fundamental to how we think about the past, and how we connect it in both real and imaginative terms to our present and then the future.

After completing a BA (Hons) degree in history from Newnham College, Cambridge, I went on to study the history of dress (MA and PhD) at the Courtauld Institute of Art. This book is the fruition of many years of thinking about the links and relationships between history and dress history, in particular the importance of dress *in* history. The subject of fashion and class could have been approached in a number of different ways from the one adopted here; needless to say, this study only touches the tip of the proverbial iceberg. I do not offer a global perspective; class as a concept for describing social and cultural stratification first emerged in specific historical circumstances and was, as I argue in this study, the result of a particular pattern of economic growth and industrialisation in Britain. In that respect I adopt, unfashionably perhaps, but also unapologetically, a micro- rather than a macro-historical approach.

Frances Arnold at Bloomsbury Publishing has been the most encouraging and supportive editorial director any academic writer could wish for. Heartfelt thanks to her and also to her wonderfully efficient and helpful editorial assistant Yvonne Thouroude. Thank you to Oliver Douglas and Caroline Benson for kind permission to use the images from the Museum of English Rural Life, University of Reading; to Nicolas Bell and Sandy Paul at Trinity College Library and to the Master and Fellows of Trinity College, Cambridge, for permitting me to reproduce here the images from the Arthur Munby Collection; and finally, to Nicola Herbert for making it possible for me to include the images from the Marks & Spencer Company Archive at the University of Leeds.

Introduction

An end of apparel is the distinguishing or differencing of persons.
                          Richard Allestree, *The Whole Duty of Man*[1]

It is hard to imagine such a different time and place, when the etiquette of 'hat honour' required men of lowly status to remove their headwear for superiors, while those of a more 'elevated' social position could remain with their heads covered in the presence of persons of lesser status. But in the eighteenth century an onlooker would have been able easily to identify different social position by dress – both the clothing itself and the manner in which it was worn. The same could not necessarily be said of the casual observer of any early-twenty-first-century gathering, with casual 'hoodies', along with joggers and trainers worn by many of all classes and ages for much of the time, and, more often than not, with the hoods pulled up over the head.

While keeping in mind Alexandra Warwick and Dani Cavallaro's important question, 'where does the body end and where does dress begin?',[2] in this study, dress is defined principally as clothing, referring when it is relevant to accessories, hairstyles, jewellery and the total 'look'. The history of shoes, for example, reveals how these essential items are inextricably linked to notions of class, but that this relationship didn't remain static: the Venetian chopine (derived from a style so popular in fifteenth-century Spain that the country's cork supplies were almost exhausted) became a symbol of status and wealth (Figure I.1).[3] Later, in seventeenth- and eighteenth-century Europe red heels were worn only by the privileged classes,[4] not unlike the red soles and heels of contemporary Christian Loboutin shoes which, with their high price tag, consequently have an 'exclusive' customer! In the past, shoes made of precious metals and fabulously decorated were often associated with wealth and

Figure I.1 Pair of chopines covered in green silk velvet and cream silk ribbon, the platform sole trimmed in gold lace with hobnails, gold braid edging and with a tassel below the open toe. Italian, *ca.* 1550–1650. Accession no. 2009.300.1494. Courtesy of the Metropolitan Museum of Art, New York, www.metmuseum.org (Brooklyn Museum Costume Collection at The Metropolitan Museum of Art, Gift of the Brooklyn Museum, 2009; Gift of Herman Delman, 1955).

prestige.[5] On the other hand, the consequences of having no shoes and going barefoot in the winter are described by Frank McCourt in his 1996 memoir *Angela's Ashes*.[6] By contrast an excess of materialism was evidenced by the wealth of former Philippines first lady Imelda Marcus made manifest by her shoe obsession.[7]

Fashion and Class begins at the end of the eighteenth century, and is, on the one hand, about how dress became a reflection – dim or otherwise – of perceptions of class, and, on the other hand, about how dress itself contributed to the evolution of how we understand the idea of class. It is something of a challenge to project ourselves into a world in which fabric and clothing were not the disposable, throwaway, transient commodities they often are today but, rather, prior to the advent of fast-changing fashions, more permanent symbols of economic and social status. Indeed, it was often the very fact that their cut and fabric were perceived as 'unchanging' that conferred on their wearers the association of rank and stability in otherwise turbulent times. However, as early as the 1660s and 1670s, Edwina Ehrman has shown how the importance of novelty in textiles for the very wealthy was evidenced by the high turnover of patterns and colours. France rationalised the design of woven silks made in Lyon by instituting a system of annual change. The system enabled the design, marketing and manufacture of the complex, high-quality silks for which Lyon was renowned to be more logically planned and gave each year's designs valuable kudos. At the same time Lyon's reputation for fashion leadership was bolstered by the reorganisation of dress worn at the court of Louis XIV (1638–1715). Each year fresh silks were to be ordered for the royal wardrobe and the old discarded (Figure I.2).[8]

In the eighteenth century, it was not possible to buy clothing 'off the peg' in the way we so easily do today. Rather, a large amount of time and resources – either one's own or other people's – went into the making and care of clothes at all social levels. Costly fabrics were used and reused so that even when styles changed, garments were habitually reworked, or, in the case of the clothing of the poor, worn and used as rags (as we understand that term today) and eventually, when no more life could be eked out of them, consigned to the manure heap. Ironic then that clothing in the twenty-first century, once past its short-lived usefulness as 'fashion', frequently ends up in landfill. But given the non-biodegradable nature of synthetic textiles such as polyester and nylon (only a small proportion of which are recycled) the transience of fashion itself – in terms of cut and styling – can be contrasted to the longevity of the fabrics from which it is created, the latter consigned to inhabit the soil for generations to come.

By the nineteenth century the annual fashion 'system' described earlier was embedded in the promotion of women's fashion. From this time, in Britain and Western Europe, fashion – it is generally assumed – was 'democratised' as a result of technological and sociocultural change. Not only has fashion actively assisted in breaking down social stratification, but it is also a visible sign of the democratisation of the social hierarchy that we take for granted today. In other words, fashion seems to be available to all, with no obvious restrictions, let alone those imposed by the sumptuary legislation of the past. The latter attempted to control the type of fabric permissible or the specific styles or colours of garments to be worn by a person of a particular social and economic status; clothing and fabric therefore assisted in maintaining the social hierarchy and status quo. The mass production of affordable ready-to-wear clothing

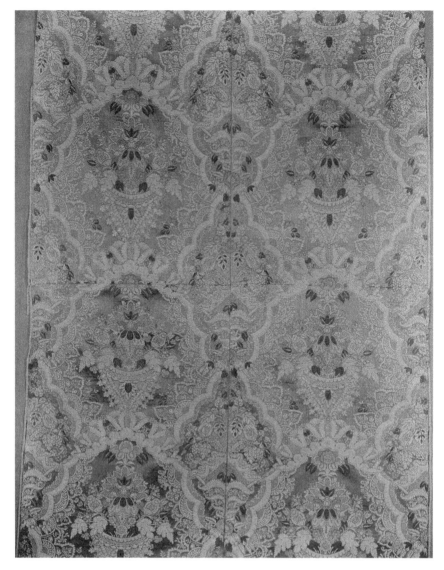

Figure I.2 Fragment of silk, French, *ca.* 1720. Accession no. 38.30.2. Courtesy of the Metropolitan Museum of Art, New York, www.metmuseum.org (Fletcher Fund, 1938).

and the consequent demise of made-to-measure clothing are both cause and effect of this complex two-way process of democratisation. But it was not ever thus. Prior to the emergence of class as a term defining social stratification, perceptions of 'rank' and 'status' strongly influenced people's 'choice' of clothing; by the mid-nineteenth century, however, 'class' had become the more usual turn of phrase. But whatever the changing relationships between rank, status, class and fashion over time, they testify to the ever-present notion that a sense of hierarchy is part of the human psyche and that this is articulated and communicated via appearance.

This book explores the notion of class in relation to a discussion of significant influences on fashion: politics, technology, social democratisation and mass retailing, design and, finally, ethical considerations and sustainability, in relation to the production and consumption of clothing. Using a broadly chronological structure, it is arranged thematically. Individual chapters – though these do not assume that the topic being considered should be studied in isolation – provide case studies that exemplify and illustrate these influences in turn. While class has evolved over time and can be defined variously in political, economic, social and cultural terms, my intention is, rather than attempting one static meaning, to consider the ways in which, from the mid-eighteenth century until the late twentieth and into the twenty-first centuries, changing fashions were closely related to evolving notions of class. More elusively perhaps, I want also to interrogate the idea of class in relation to changing clothing styles alongside the waxing and waning popularity of particular *fabrics*; to ask, in other words, how fashion in its broadest sense both reflects and contributes to the idea of class. As Susan Vincent points out in her exploration of elite styles in the period 1550–1670, 'Objects ... do not just express culture, they also create it.'[9] And although such meanings are relative and change over time, they are made real and intelligible only in relation to other people's styles of dress, in other words by virtue of being *different*. The social and economic historian E. P. Thompson in *The Making of the English Working Class* (1963) showed how class evolves from difference.[10] To be different one has to be set apart from something or someone else. Social class, says writer Marilynne Robinson in *When I Was a Child I Read Books* (2012), 'makes culture a system of signs and passwords, more or less entirely without meaning except as it identifies groups and subgroups'.[11] Dress is part of culture and it contributes therefore to that 'system' by helping to identify different social groups. I want to explore the ways in which fabrics and styles have distinguished one class from another, but, conversely, and over time, how they may also have disguised those distinctions.

One example here serves to illustrate the ways in which dress and fabric define status and class, but reveals how such definitions change over time. In the 1990s, what, if anything, did ripped black clothing – for example, an expensive designer item by Zandra Rhodes (b. 1940) – tell us about class? In the seventeenth-century Dutch Republic, the combination of clothing that was black but also torn (if that combination had existed) would have had contradictory associations. On the one hand, black was an indication of wealth and status: the Union of Utrecht (1579) brought together seven provinces of the northern Netherlands, thereby winning independence from Spain, with Amsterdam becoming an important cultural centre gaining ascendancy over Antwerp. A proliferation of portraits evidences the culture and patronage of

Figure I.3 *Portrait of a Man*, probably a member of the Van Beresteyn Family, by Rembrandt van Rijn (1606–1669), 1632. Oil on canvas, 111.8 × 88.9 cm. Accession no. 29.100.3. Courtesy of the Metropolitan Museum of Art, New York, www. metmuseum.org (H. O. Havemeyer Collection, Bequest of Mrs. H. O. Havemeyer, 1929).

arts in this period and in particular of the Regent class – stately and powerful merchants and magistrates (mostly Protestant) – whose fashions were, perhaps ironically, influenced by Spanish dress. Formal black clothing, often with the addition of elaborate lace ruffs, was the order of the day as seen in many paintings by Rembrandt van Rijn (1606–1669): portraits of a man and woman (*ca.* 1632) (Figures I.3 and I.4). Frans Hals (1582–1666) also dressed a number of his sitters in dark fabric, decorated with embroidery and lace, but in a more informal manner (Figure I.5). These images are starkly different from those painted by Elias Boursse (1631–1672), such as *A Woman Cooking* (1656), in which the subject of the painting wears a garment (different from a ruff) called a 'collerette' or 'kletje', typically worn by seventeenth-century

Figure I.4 *Portrait of a Woman*, probably a member of the Van Beresteyn Family, by Rembrandt van Rijn (1606–1669), 1632. Oil on canvas, 111.8 × 88.9 cm. Accession no. 29.100.4. Courtesy of the Metropolitan Museum of Art, New York, www. metmuseum.org (H. O. Havemeyer Collection, Bequest of Mrs. H. O. Havemeyer, 1929).

Figure I.5 *Portrait of a Man*, possibly Nicolaes Pietersz Duyst van Voorhout, by Frans Hals (1582/3–1666), *ca.* 1636–8. Oil on canvas, 80.6 × 66 cm. Accession no. 49.7.33. Courtesy of the Metropolitan Museum of Art, New York, www.metmuseum.org (The Jules Bache Collection, 1949).

working people. Rank and status as defined by clothing seem to be clearly communicated in the case of the paintings of Rembrandt, Hals and Boursse. But the ripped black clothing of the late twentieth century could be 'read' in a very different way because status and social position are no longer fashion's main terms of reference. The relationship between fashion and class is both culturally specific and has changed over time.

Mending would have rescued all but the most disintegrated of garments; rips and holes have, more often than not, indicated extreme poverty in most periods and contexts. Like other 'modifications', mended or patched garments have come in and gone out of favour – often a sign of poverty, their status during the Second World War changed, evidenced by the Board of Trade's 'Make Do and Mend' campaign: 'A neatly patched garment is something to be proud of nowadays rather than a sign of poverty.'[12] But the trend in the 1990s for deconstruction and grunge (Chapter 7) had a powerful effect, subverting or even reversing such associations. So, a black, ripped and torn item of clothing – Valerie Mendes made the point that such an item is no longer confined to the poor and underprivileged[13] – that can only be afforded by an elite in terms of financial status, therefore, defies traditional fashion and class associations. Conversely an affordable suit designed by a high-profile designer – such as an article of 'designer' clothing sold at high street prices, or a suit sold under the Utility label – likewise overturned traditional associations between designers and elites.

So, if class still exists today in Britain, is it in part defined by particular ways of dressing? In what ways has fashion itself assisted the breakdown of class barriers, and is there a place for the notion of class in the twenty-first century as a tool for analysis of society in terms of visual appearance? In relation to the Early Modern period, Susan Vincent refers to apparel as 'a cultural production of the privileged' and while clothing may not have the 'declared centrality to the realisation of power, wealth, status and gender' that it has had in previous periods,[14] it still has the power to define meaning, whether in terms of practicality and utility, allure and fashion, identity and gender (or non-gender), religion and culture, or, and in relation to this study, *class*.

This book focuses on the two hundred or so years from the late eighteenth to the late twentieth century. It is not of course immune from the biases that result from its having been written from the perspective of the early decades of the twenty-first century, which have seen enormous changes – brought about partly by the internet – in the ways in which fashion is produced, retailed and consumed. In 1750 Britain was also on the cusp of radical technological and social change heralding a new social structure based predominantly on labour relations and whose best-known critics – Karl Marx (1818–1883) and Friedrich Engels (1820–1895) – later saw it as being largely the result of an exploitative factory system, in which one class came to rule over another. And it is not insignificant that in this new system, textiles, and especially cotton, played a central role. This interpretation – though simplified here – is of importance to the evolution of the argument developed over the chapters that follow, which will ultimately bring us to where we are today. In post-industrial and (relatively) affluent Western societies, while we rarely talk about rank and status, we still, however, refer to class although its relationship with fashion has become more complex.

This symbiosis between class and fashion has metamorphosed over time. And in this study, I offer just one perspective on that journey of transition. Britain is not viewed in isolation; rather with American, European and Japanese cross-currents increasingly felt as a consequence of improved communications of all kinds and as the world began to become smaller in how it was perceived both in geographical and cultural terms. But in order to do justice to the particularity of its social structure, my focus is unapologetically on Britain and, in particular, England. Individual historical circumstances shape the evolution of class structure in any one context and therefore generalisation across different historical experience can be unhelpful, except for purposes of comparison.

The notion of class is complex and has been contested by historians. Is it a meaningful description of social stratification in the twenty-first century? Robert Colls points out that while ' "class" as a great organising concept has all but left the academy it has not, of course, left the history'.[15] Although neither a detailed history of class per se, nor an historical exploration of different definitions of what the term has meant or what it currently means, Chapter 1 explores the historical evolution of the notion of class, from its origins as an essentially Marxist definition to one that has, almost imperceptibly, become a more general way of describing social stratification that can be related to a discussion about the politics, production, retailing and consumption and design of fashion. It considers the ways in which notions of class and taste were woven into theories about fashionable change and consumption. In the context of the French Revolution, Chapter 2 addresses political revolution and the ways in which ideas surrounding privilege and democracy were caught up in the politics of fashion in France in the last decade of the eighteenth century. But politics cannot be considered in isolation and Chapters 3 and 4 consider the technological growth of the textile industry in England and the ways in which class identity and conflict were expressed through clothing and dress. The impact of industrialisation and the technological 'revolution' of the late eighteenth and nineteenth centuries – in particular as the latter affected the cotton industry and trends towards mass production and consumption – are also explored here. The fictional work of Fanny Burney and Jane Austen provide a useful 'context' for the ensuing impact of economic change described by those authors considering the 'Condition of England' question in the nineteenth century. I examine the extent to which these changes over time brought about a degree of class levelling or whether in fact the industrial system as it developed by the mid-nineteenth century actually intensified class antagonism in the way that novelists such as Elizabeth Gaskell, Charles Kingsley and George Eliot believed.

The theme of democratisation is developed in Chapters 5 and 6 in relation to the development of ready-to-wear clothing and the contribution of high-street retailers in the late nineteenth and twentieth centuries: pioneering department stores and, in particular, chain stores such as C&A and Marks & Spencer and, in the second half of the twentieth century, boutique and youth fashion outlets. It is in this context that the roles of design and the designer in more global terms are discussed in Chapter 7, both in the provision of luxury and elite clothing, but also in relation to the evolution of ready-to-wear clothing and the increasingly visible role played by designers in creating ranges for the high-street and products destined for wider consumption than via traditional channels, either couture or ready-to-wear. Finally, I touch the surface of the complex relationship between sustainability and the mass consumption of fashion towards the close of the twentieth century and at the start of the twenty-first century. Discussion of the consumption of throwaway, 'fast' fashion segues into one which considers the ways in which initiatives towards a more sustainable approach to recycling, mending and 'local' sourcing might facilitate a model of clothing production and consumption in which class might ultimately become both an irrelevance and an anomaly.

1

What's in a name? The language of class in relation to fashion and fabrics

Adopting a sociological approach, Diana Crane revealed how, in pre-industrial societies, clothing indicated very precisely a person's position in the social structure, revealing not only status and gender, but frequently occupation, religious affiliation and regional origin. However, as Western societies industrialised, the effect of social stratification on clothing 'behaviour' was such that 'the expression of class and gender took precedence over the communication of other types of social information'.[1] This chapter explores how the evolution of the notion of class – originating from an essentially Marxist definition to one that has, almost imperceptibly, become a more general way of describing social stratification – can be related to a discussion about the politics, production, design, retailing and consumption of fashion. It also considers the ways in which ideas around class and taste were woven into theories that aim to explain changes in fashion. Often useful as insights into the time in which they were written, such theories offer, however, limited and mostly 'top-down' models of fashionable change.

Class is widely accepted as a quintessentially British fact of life, 'a heritage and language that we can all share'.[2] Although definitions of class have evolved over time, the term endures in English common parlance and informs how we see ourselves in social, cultural and economic relations to others. The decline in the numbers engaged in domestic service in the first half of the twentieth century and of those working in the British textile industries over the course of the latter half of the twentieth and into the twenty-first centuries (due in part to outsourcing by powerful retailers) and the closing of mines, steelworks and shipyards – in other words the demise of those workplaces in which the British working classes were, to use historian E. P. Thompson's phrase, 'made' – have together led to a decrease in the number of people who could, strictly speaking, be described as working class. In fact, it has been argued that white working-class men are probably 'the most forgotten and ill-considered class in contemporary Britain'.[3] However, the rise and dominance of service industries and the professions has resulted in the 'middle classes' (using the term loosely) gaining ascendancy in terms of relative numbers.

In the twentieth century, changes in the labour market and in occupations were not alone in impacting directly on class structures; there were other factors, such as wider social change and a degree of class levelling brought about by two world wars, greater equality for women and the impact of the labour movement and trade unions. Following the General Strike of 1928, the 1930s have been identified as a period of 'class struggle', with the Transport and General Workers' Union (TGWU) becoming Britain's largest union by 1939.[4] The textile industry continued to be an arena for industrial dispute, just as it had been almost a century earlier: mass production conducted on assembly lines in factories was a radically new development in the 1930s. In 1931 workers engaged in hosiery production at Leicester's Wolsey plant walked out en masse.[5] However, class-consciousness was, arguably, considerably denuded with the erosion of the distinction between the 'deserving' and 'undeserving' poor demonstrated by Aneurin Bevan's support for universal welfare provision (not 'policed' by a means test) and Clement Attlee's Labour government (1945–51).[6] The latter saw the inauguration of a comprehensive welfare state and compulsory free secondary education for all children aged between eleven and fifteen. The provisions of the 1936 Education Act raised the school leaving age to fifteen in principle, but this was postponed until the 1944 Education Act was implemented in 1947. In 1972 the school leaving age was raised to sixteen.

Yet even with (relative) social levelling over the course of the second half of the twentieth century, the early twenty-first century saw continued material inequality, in a society in which the consumption of 'stuff' was heralded as the measure of (economic) well-being. Class today is perhaps less about political power, educational attainment or cultural identity, but more about how *much* we own, and the means by which we *get* what we own. Accordingly, the recession and cuts of the early twenty-first century have reaffirmed the relevance of class in contemporary Britain in which the richest 10 per cent are said to have become richer and the poorest 10 per cent poorer.

Even so, in the 1990s politicians of the left and right heralded the emergence of a classless society. Suzanne Moore, in an article in the *Guardian*, wrote: 'The unleashing of the market has continued to undermine the post-war settlement, a way of organising society in which people identified themselves by class. Technology has further ruptured this class identification as people cluster in networks and not hierarchies.'[7] But *perceptions* of class are significant, with the polls suggesting in the early twenty-first century that more than half of British people still considered themselves to be working class.[8] 'Class', observes Danny Dorling, 'is not simply your relation to the means of production, or a quantity that can be determined for you when you answer a few survey questions. It is also who you think you are.'[9] Class is very much part of our collective historical consciousness, the latter both evidencing and perpetuating its existence. Furthermore, the history of the use of the term 'class' also evidences the way in which language 'constructs our understanding of the world'.[10]

Perceptions of class have therefore clearly mutated over time. However, for most of the period covered by this study, the working classes, broadly defined, dominated in terms of sheer numbers. It has been calculated that by the end of the nineteenth century, they constituted the overwhelming majority in England (85 per cent) when compared with those in the United States (82 per cent) and France (73 per cent).[11] In the early twentieth century the so-called traditional working class – everyone who worked with their hands, whether actually in or out of work – still constituted the vast majority of Britons. Even by mid-century, if we include manual workers and their families, domestic servants and lower grade clerical workers – typists, secretaries, office boys, messengers – the proportion has been calculated to be more than three-quarters and more than half as late as 1991.[12] Of these, domestic servants – singled out in terms of dress because they often came into close contact with notions of high fashion and yet had to wear unpopular caps and aprons – constituted the largest single group of working people in Britain in 1910 and 1923.[13]

Social classes are not monolithic, however, and we need to be wary of using the concept too simplistically. The terms 'working', 'middle' and 'upper' class(es) should, strictly speaking, be used in the plural if we are to take account of the nuances existing within any one of these designations. In the nineteenth century, for example, the working class comprised skilled labourers at the top and criminals and paupers at the bottom, with a multitude in between.[14] In his novel *The Rainbow* (1915), D. H. Lawrence, the son of a Nottinghamshire miner, referring probably to the 1880s, describes Will Brangwen – himself working class – tempted away from his wife one evening after a football match in Nottingham when he meets Jennie: 'He noted the common accent. It pleased him. He knew what class she came of. Probably she was a warehouse lass. He was glad she was a common girl.'[15] Brangwen's startling class-consciousness illustrates the complexity of social stratification as well as the matter-of-fact articulation of class definitions and identities. Virginia Woolf's description of the working classes in their 'hideous clothes' is also unashamedly class-conscious – elsewhere she speaks of the 'shoddy old fetters of class'[16] – but her perspective was from a *middle-class* standpoint, and her writing has a very different impact on the reader compared with that of Lawrence.

Evolution of the term 'class'

This study covers the period from the latter decades of the eighteenth century to the first two decades of the twenty-first century. The former saw the dual impact on fashion and style as a result of the American Revolution of 1776 and the French Revolution of 1789. However, class acquired currency in the nineteenth century and is specifically associated with the intensive industrialisation of that period which went hand in hand with the evolution of the British factory system. (While the middle-class characters of Jane Austen's novels are very much aware of class, we will see that her world is far away from the industrial 'context' of Elizabeth Gaskell's and Charles Dickens's novels.) The latter created a new social structure based on the exploitation of large numbers of workers and their labour by a relatively small managerial and factory-owning elite: precisely the kind of model described by Elizabeth Gaskell in her novels *Mary Barton* (1848) and *North and South* (1855) and satirised in Charles Dickens's *Hard Times* (1854). The conflict in interests of, on the one hand, factory operatives, struggling to work and support themselves and their families and, on the other, the factory managers and owners – who, with few exceptions, were more interested in making a profit based on a crude cash-nexus model – lies at the centre of all of these novels. These opposing interests were famously described by E. P. Thompson in his pioneering account of the evolution of class and class-consciousness, *The Making of the English Working Class* (1963):

> Class happens, when some men, as a result of common experiences (inherited or shared) feel and articulate the identity of their interests as between themselves, and as against other men whose interests are different from (and usually opposed to) theirs.[17]

According to Peter Laslett, in pre-industrial society, there was a large number of status groups (the number of people enjoying or enduring the same social status) but only one body of persons capable of concerted action over the whole area of society, 'only one class in fact'. 'Class' is defined by Laslett as 'a number of people banded together in the exercise of collective power, political and economic'.[18] According to the Oxford English Dictionary, its use in regard to a social division or grouping does not appear until 1772. Until then, 'estate', 'order', 'rank' and 'degree' (terms that originated in medieval times) continued to be used to describe social positions. The use of the word 'class' is therefore historically associated with the Industrial Revolution and the rise of capitalism, making it somewhat anachronistic to apply it to earlier systems of class division.[19] The idea of class thus evolved with a Marxist tradition of historical interpretation that analyses and explains labour relations as resulting from *industrial* capitalism. Of course, social stratification had existed in England long before the industrialisation of the nineteenth century, but notions of 'orders' and 'ranks' were based on fundamentally different historical circumstances which had evolved over the centuries and were often closely related to patterns of landownership, and, in turn, the latter's relationship to the monarchy. The nobility – including titles from earl down to gentry – constituted the most powerful but also the minority in terms of numbers. Meanwhile, according to Gregory King's well-known analysis of the structure of English society for 1688, the largest group of families in England was made up of 'cottagers and paupers': 400,000 out of 1,350,000.[20] By contrast, of all the people alive in Tudor and Stuart England, at most one out of twenty (i.e. 5 per cent) belonged to the gentry and above.[21] This hierarchical structure was justified by the widely held belief that the order of society was ordained by God. Modes of dress, as the most visible indications of social status in the pre-industrial era, were therefore seen and 'read' in direct relation to that structure and this justified the sumptuary legislation of the Early Modern period (Chapter 2).

If the development of class from the late eighteenth century as a category for defining opposing interests and relative economic status testified to 'pervasive inequality',[22] ultimately the pre-existing demarcations that distinguished people visually gradually broke down: in other words, class would ultimately create, if not classlessness, then at least a degree of democratisation in dress. Historian Neil McKendrick considers dress to be 'the most public manifestation of the blurring of class divisions which was so commented on' in the eighteenth century.[23] Here is something of a paradox, then – that fashion can be seen as both a powerful indicator of class, but also as the means for its dissolution. Class, derived from economic difference, had – and has – repercussions for cultural and social differences too. Furthermore, the factory system of the early nineteenth century evolved in relation to, significantly, the *textile* industry and, in particular, the cotton industry (Chapter 3). The production of cotton that was derived from West Indian slavery – the most extreme example of a system of oppression of one class by another – led eventually to the liberation of slaves. Likewise, the social conditions of workers in the cotton spinning and weaving industries of the late eighteenth and nineteenth centuries (the British textile factory system was often actually compared to West Indian slavery) were so notorious that their regulation would lead ultimately to the slow disappearance of the class system as it had evolved up to that point. And so perhaps there is some 'historic justice' in the fact that the cotton on which both the slave trade and the factory system depended contributed, ultimately, to a blurring of class distinctions signalled by fabric and clothing.

Fashion as a concept and aesthetic framework as well as actual material clothing is both produced *and* consumed and this gives it a particular relevance to shifting definitions of class. As we shall see, the history of the *production* of textiles, especially that of the British cotton industry, has traditionally provided a focus for economic historians analysing the process of industrialisation from the mid-eighteenth century, but the history of the consumption of those textile goods and of fashion more generally only became a focus for study by historians in the late twentieth century. The rise in consumption 'as an arena in which people's desires and hopes are centred' has brought about a shift from production to consumption 'as the new basis of structural divisions and unities in society, as well as of people's conceptions of themselves and the social order'.[24]

Ben Fine and Ellen Leopold have written effectively of the 'false' dichotomy between production and consumption, considering the fashion system to be a 'dual' system of provision, defined as the 'interrelationship between highly fragmented forms of production and equally diverse and often volatile patterns of demand'. Fashion, they argue, is a 'hybrid' subject, since it is both a 'cultural phenomenon' and 'an aspect of manufacturing with the accent on production technology'. This dual aspect of the fashion system partly explains why it has been 'a difficult subject to accommodate within a tradition of economic history in which the histories of consumption and production plough largely separate furrows'.[25] The division between the respective histories of production and consumption has resulted in a 'top downwards' perspective on the history of dress with lip-service paid to acknowledging the history of 'ordinary fashion'. The work of Ted Polhemus, in particular his *Streetstyle* (first published 1994), sought to address the 'top downwards' bias of much fashion history by focusing on the ways in which street styles since the mid-twentieth century have subverted the traditional 'monopoly' of high fashion.[26]

The premise on which the whole concept of class is based and therefore the extent to which class is an effective and relevant descriptive term became the source of debate among historians at the end of the twentieth century. As a consequence the edifice of English Marxist social history has been subjected to analysis, with class coming under 'increasing scrutiny as a means of explaining both the present and the past'.[27] Further, 'a common, socio-economic condition as proletarians or dependent, manual, waged workers, would in fact seem central to any definition of what "working class" might mean, as would a shared perception of this common condition'.[28] 'If class has a rival', explains Patrick Joyce (in terms of popular conceptions of the social order), 'it is perhaps that of "populism", of "the people"'.[29] In the end, however, Joyce concludes that 'numerous text books and monographs continue to be written in which classes are still historical actors, albeit without their Marxist roles'.[30] So while the centrality of class as the focus of this study acknowledges the debt to Marxist accounts of the history of society in the nineteenth century, it also assumes a broader and less circumscribed definition of class, one in which classes are not considered to be either monolithic or static entities.

Working-class dress

During the period covered by the greater part of this book working-class people outnumbered any other social class. However, a definition of the term has continued to exercise historians. Patrick Curry offers a thoughtful consideration of the criticism levelled towards E. P. Thompson for too readily using the term 'working class' for many different types of working people and in particular for assuming that these people had just one struggle.[31] So, in an attempt to do fuller justice to the complexity and diversity of nineteenth-century society, it is useful to mention here R. S. Neale's (1970s) model. For the period 1800–50, Neale avoids using the conventional three-class model, offering instead a five-class model, in which he splits the working class as follows:

> Working Class A: industrial proletariat in factory areas, workers in domestic industries, collective and non-deferential and wanting government intervention to protect rather than liberate them.
>
> Working Class B: agricultural labourers, other low-paid non-factory urban labourers, domestic servants, urban poor, most working-class women whether from working class A or B households, deferential and dependent.[32]

Neale thus distinguishes the agricultural labourer and other groups from the industrial (factory-based) worker, whose interests became increasingly divergent as the nineteenth century progressed. While useful in offering a more detailed and nuanced alternative to the traditional three-class model for describing English society in the period, Neale's model does not make a generic distinction between rural and urban interests. The balance between the 'rural' and the 'urban' shifted significantly from mid-century onwards with the census of 1851 providing the quantitative evidence that, for the first time, the population was more urban than rural.[33]

Whether we can truly talk of a *rural working class* in the second half of the nineteenth century depends on the extent to which agrarian capitalism actually took hold in the countryside and the ways in which the rural labouring population therefore constituted a rural 'proletariat'. Defined at its most basic, proletarianisation here suggests that the land is expropriated by a capitalist elite, leaving the labourer nothing to sell but his or her labour power while reliant on the forces of the market for work, housing and food.[34] Historians have analysed the combined impact of enclosure, mechanisation, the breakdown of traditional paternalistic relations between employer (farmer) and labourer and the onset of agrarian capitalism, but they are divided in their conclusions. G. E. Mingay, for example, assumes the existence of a rural proletariat although he avoids offering a strict definition of the term. Describing the rural proletariat as a shrinking one in the period 1871–1911 – when the proportion of the national workforce engaged in agriculture nearly halved – he adds, somewhat unhelpfully, that still 'it remained a proletariat'.[35] Meanwhile Howard Newby argues that 'by the early nineteenth century, the village population … had become primarily a proletarian one'.[36] For Eric Hobsbawm and George Rudé, 'the typical English agriculturalist was a hired man, a rural proletarian'.[37] Alun Howkins, however, uses the term more cautiously, observing that although there were what could be described as proletarians in particular rural areas of England – on the large arable farms of the eastern counties, for example – a simplistic picture of homogeneous agrarian capitalism should be challenged: 'I for one', he asserts, 'am certain that we need to reinstate peasant into the vocabulary of rural history in England.'[38]

So, while there is no consensus on whether the appellation of proletarianism can be attached, we *can* ask about the degree to which rural protest – machine-breaking and incendiarism that culminated in the Swing Riots of 1830, the eviction of the Tolpuddle Martyrs in 1834 and later attempts at rural trade unionism from the 1870s – can be considered to be indicative or causative of political consciousness and class solidarity among rural workers. On this issue there is no agreement either. Whereas Hobsbawm and Rudé view the 1830 Swing Riots as an expression of rural class protest, historians have also expressed surprise at the labourer's passivity, given that their economic plight in terms of wages and general living conditions was so dire. Studies of rural popular culture such as Ian Dyck's analysis of the subject matter of cottage songs of the period add a further dimension to the parameters of this debate.

As Dyck observes: 'If the songs of the farm workers do not permit us to assign a precise date to the birth of class consciousness in the rural world, they do permit us to say that the labourers were conscious of class experience as early as the 1820s.'[39] Meanwhile for E. P. Thompson, the English working class was in the making by the 1830s (some have criticised that this is too early); embedded by the 1890s; central by the 1940s; and at the post-industrial crossroads by the 1960s.[40] Discussion of the role of fabric and clothing in the following chapters contributes a new dimension to this debate.

The idea of a unified working class and especially the term 'proletarian' do scant justice to the diverse and fragmented nature of the labour force in general in the nineteenth century. Patrick Joyce concludes that the term ' "working class" is exceedingly tenuous as an adequate description' and 'can be defended only with much qualification'.[41] But on the other hand it often becomes meaningful when used in relation to the fabrics and clothing of particular classes to distinguish them from others. In consideration of the actual language in which contemporaries talked about the social order, 'class' is used in interesting contexts. For example, the writer William Cobbett refers to 'labouring people' in Kent and to smock-frocks in relation to this 'class'.[42] In 1867 parliamentary commissioner Mr Stanhope (for the county of Cheshire) was appointed to enquire into the employment of children, young persons and women in agriculture and refers unequivocally to the term 'working classes'.[43] Such references to class often carry with them associations with a distinctive style of clothing or type of fabric. A former agricultural labourer, writer Alexander Somerville refers to different categories of the social hierarchy in terms of their (distinctive) clothing. Rather than simply describing what different classes wore, the type of clothing is used interchangeably with the actual groups of people, thus 'landlords' are 'frock-coats' and 'labourers' are 'smock-frocks'.[44] These clothing associations serve not just as visual description but can be metaphors for the social and economic roles played by different classes and occupations. However, Richard Jefferies comments on changes afoot in the second half of the nineteenth century and on a degree of class levelling, such that the Wiltshire labourers in 1872 'are much better clothed now than formerly', adding that there has been a reversal in the clothing normally associated with particular classes:

Corduroy trousers and slops are the usual style. Smock-frocks are going out of use. … Almost every labourer has his Sunday suit, very often really good clothes, sometimes glossy black, with the regulation 'chimney-pot'. Since labour is become so expensive it has become a common remark among the farmers that the labourer will go to church in broadcloth and the masters in smock-frocks.[45]

Meanwhile, social historian Paul Pickering's work directly addresses the significance of clothing and fabric in the characterisation and evolution of working-class identity in the Chartist movement of the 1830s and 1840s. He considers the significance of the appearance of the Chartist leader Feargus O'Connor addressing Chartist meetings in a fustian suit, concluding that this was 'one of the most significant public declarations of the early 1840s: it was a statement of class without words'.[46] Similarly, the agricultural trade union leader Joseph Arch describes in his autobiography his own choice of dress, for example, smock-frock, fustian and moleskins, as a badge of identity with the working classes (Figures 1.1 and 1.2).[47] Discussion of class – its significance both as a tool for analysis and as a term denoting social

Figure 1.1 Detail of white linen smock-frock, nineteenth century, Massingham Collection. Accession no. 51/258. Courtesy of the Museum of English Rural Life, University of Reading.

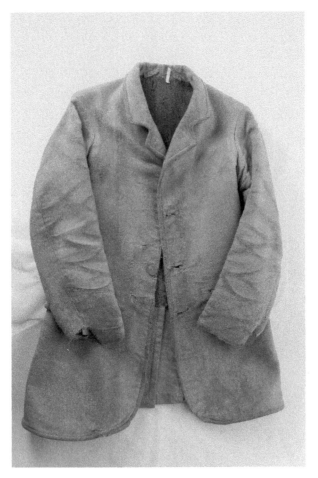

Figure 1.2 Coat of fustian, purportedly bought from a Hampshire shepherd in 1914. Accession no.74/4. Courtesy of the Museum of English Rural Life, University of Reading.

relationships – throws light on how contemporaries perceived themselves in relation to others and reveals that fabric and clothing communicate much more than occupation, economic situation, social status, aesthetic choice/ lack of choice and so on.

Therefore, a narrative that considers discussion of working-class dress offers a more inclusive and balanced perspective than one which focuses primarily on the clothing of the elite and middle classes. Not only is it useful to show how working-class dress was distinguished from, say, middle-class styles, but it can also be enlightening to highlight the variations *within* it, such as the distinctions made here between 'urban' and 'rural' in the second half of the nineteenth century.

Fashion and change

Class relationships, especially those in which the upper and middle classes are perceived to influence or dominate aesthetic 'value' and 'taste', lie at the heart of some influential analyses and explanations of fashionable change. These stem from a predominantly 'top-down' approach to historical causation and a long-held assumption that those who hold power also hold cultural influence. Thus, sumptuary legislation of the Early Modern period is more easily understood in the context of hierarchical divisions in which the idea of 'apeing one's betters' was derided because it challenged the accepted order of society. And the well-used term 'dressing up' implies appropriation of the clothing of those 'higher' *up* the social scale. Referring to Henry James's novella *The Turn of the Screw*, published in the final decade of the nineteenth century, Peter Davidson speaks of the 'revulsion at the servant usurping the place of his master, the servant in his master's clothes'.[48] In Walter de la Mare's short story *Crewe* (1942), the manservant sitting in a first-class waiting room dressed in the coat of his dead master fills the scene with mystery and unsettles the reader. To contemporaries this was the 'correct' order of things in reverse.

Dressing 'down' to imitate those below one on the social scale could, on the contrary, be deemed acceptable: on the eve of the First World War, an integral part of annual Christmas and Harvest Home celebrations still involved middle- and upper-class employers adopting the style of clothes more commonly worn by servants or labourers, thereby demonstrating bonds of mutual obligation.[49] In Evelyn Waugh's *Vile Bodies* (1930), 'larks' often involved the upper classes dressing as workers or the unemployed and mimicking their apparent crudities.[50] But significantly the practice of imitation in order to mock rather than to emulate was not generally reversed, or, if it was, little evidence of this seems to have survived.

The theories of Theodore Veblen (1857–1929) and Georg Simmel (1858–1918) are of particular relevance to this study as they 'explicitly linked the development of fashion to the emergence of discourses of individualism, class, civilisation and consumerism'.[51] Coining the term 'conspicuous consumption', economist and sociologist Theodore Veblen used fashion to explain Western culture's propensity to display wealth, waste and leisure through material goods and in particular women's clothing.[52] His theory of 'conspicuous waste' hinged upon an interpretation of rich and sumptuous fashionable garments, while that of 'conspicuous leisure' was explored in relation to the fact of their design being unsuitable for work activity. Influenced as they were by Marxist philosophy and by the emergence of class as a consequence of capitalist enterprise, production and consumption, Veblen's views were very much a product of his time.

Writing at the beginning of the twentieth century, philosopher and sociologist Georg Simmel saw fashion as a product of class distinction and specifically of human nature motivated by a dual and essentially contradictory impulse – to imitate but also to distinguish oneself from others. Thus, it is the effect of the dynamic play between these two batteries of apparent opposites, which are in fact two sides of the same coin. Informed by his knowledge of the role of fashion developments in the nineteenth century, Simmel thus described changes in fashion as a process of imitation of social elites by their social inferiors. The fact that lower status groups sought to acquire status by adopting the clothing of higher status groups set in motion a process of social contagion. According to Simmel, by the time a style reached the working classes, the upper classes – needing to distinguish themselves once more from those lower down the social scale – had adopted a new style (since the old style had lost its appeal). And so, argued Simmel, the cycle goes on.

Simmel thus claimed that as human beings we want to distinguish ourselves but at the same time we also want to conform. Fashion exists only insofar as one of the two poles does not ultimately prevail in the end:

> As fashion spreads, it gradually goes to its doom. The distinctiveness which in the early stages of a set fashion assures for it a certain distribution is destroyed as the fashion spreads, and as this element wanes, the fashion also is bound to die ... The attractions of both poles of the phenomena meet in fashion, and show also here that they belong together unconditionally, although, or rather because, they are contradictory in their very nature.[53]

However, the question of who did – or who did not – adopt those styles emerging from the elite is crucial for an understanding of the nature of fashion in nineteenth-century class societies. Middle-class commentators in magazines and newspapers drew their conclusions about working-class clothing from the appearance of groups who were particularly 'visible', such as servants, who, it has been widely assumed, tended – at least in the nineteenth century – either to have passed down to them the clothing of their social superiors, that is, their employers, or to have imitated their styles in a watered-down mode. However, of servants in the 1920s, it has been argued that they became symbols of a new assertive modernity fashioned by mass-produced clothes and cosmetics.[54] Associated as it is with what has become known as a 'trickle-down' effect in fashion, Simmel's 'top-down' theory does not allow for the ways in which distinction was pursued by groups other than social elites. It does not, for example, account for the adoption and origination of fabric, styles and particular clothing by working-class groups such as the French revolutionary *sans culottes* (Chapter 2) or the Chartists, for example. However, its relevance as a model for social dialectics and for the latter's interplay with fashion is significant. In this context the work of Maria Tamboukou is relevant, as she describes the encounters of French seamstresses with the bourgeois 'other' in the first half of the nineteenth century as a recurrent theme of the experience of seamstresses, since the latter were 'in constant contact with the bourgeois women whose dresses they were making'; this, she argues, evidences a facilitation of a culture of femininity that developed and transferred 'across class lines'.[55]

The work of Pierre Bourdieu proposed that the dissemination of fashion was even more complicated than the process propounded by Simmel.[56] Bourdieu described social structures as complex systems of class cultures comprising sets of cultural tastes and associated lifestyles.[57] Within social classes, individuals compete for social distinction and cultural capital on the basis of their capacity to judge the suitability of cultural products according to class-based standards of taste and manners. Cultural practices, which include both knowledge of culture and critical abilities for assessing and appreciating it, are acquired during childhood in the family and in the educational system and contribute to the reproduction of the existing social class structure: 'To the socially recognised hierarchy of the arts, and within each of them, of genres, schools or periods, corresponds a social hierarchy of the consumers. This predisposes tastes to function as markers of class.'[58] In class societies the assumption is that the dominant and most prestigious culture is that of the upper class. Although potentially enlightening for explaining how social classes and hence social structures are maintained over time, Bourdieu's theories are less useful for understanding how people respond during periods of rapid change.[59]

Veblen's and Simmel's theories are particularly interesting in the context of the time in which they were formulated; they offered a top-down approach, working on the assumption that new styles began with elites and gradually disseminated downwards in the social structure. Writing in the twentieth century – having witnessed the (relative) 'democratisation' of that century in comparison to previous ones – even the work of Bourdieu says much less about the ways in which ideas and tastes moved in other directions. Nor does it explore sufficiently, if at all, the categories of people who adopted fashionable, or retained, traditional, styles.[60] For example, describing the working classes, Bourdieu wrote that they 'make a realistic or, one might say, functionalist use of clothing. Looking for substance and function rather than form, they seek "value for money" and choose what will "last".'[61] Such theories also resulted from an essentially top-down view of society in which the upper and middle classes were perceived as the lead actors and the primary agents of historical change. And for Bourdieu at least, history was noticeably absent, not surprising perhaps given that, as he stated early on in his study, his analyses were based on a survey by questionnaire, carried out in 1963 and 1967–8, completed by a sample of 1,217 people.[62] So what happens to such theories if we attempt to redress this imbalance by considering the ways in which working-class agency in the late eighteenth and nineteenth centuries formulated a language of class that was communicated via fabric and clothing choice? Addressing this question is the focus of the following chapters.

2

The politics of fashion

By the end of the eighteenth century, the assumption that fabric and clothing indicated social and economic position in European society was deeply ingrained. Dress and fashion were highly effective communicators of social status and political allegiance. For centuries, into fabric had been woven the unwritten codes of rank, and the clothing into which it was made conveyed complex messages to others. Fashion, asserts Ferdinand Braudel, is 'an indication of deeper phenomena – of the energies, possibilities, demands and *joie de vivre* of a given society, economy and civilization'.[1] The costliness and beauty of fabric meant that the clothing of the elite signified distinction, exclusivity and camaraderie by association. Conversely, through disassociation, clothing was also a means of keeping the lower orders in what was thought to be their God-given (and lowly) place. Sumptuary law (discussed later) was, at least in part, an attempt to preserve and protect the hierarchy as communicated by dress. However, with the redefinition of those who were politically influential – such as occurred most notably during the events of the French Revolution of the late eighteenth century – the hegemony of the rich, along with their extravagant clothing, was challenged. No longer was it the prerogative of the wealthy necessarily to dominate and influence cultures of appearance, but the poorer classes exploited their own distinctive styles of dressing in order to mark themselves out from their social 'betters' and employers. Class became directly connected with subverted dress codes.

Looking back seventy years from the perspective of the late 1850s, Charles Dickens made much of the relationship between politics, fashion and class in *A Tale of Two Cities* (1859), his historical novel set in the decades leading up to the French Revolution, in which 'Monseigneur' becomes a collective noun describing the whole class of nobility against whom the working classes direct their vengeance.[2] Of Charles Darnay on his way to prison, Dickens has this to say: that 'a man in good clothes should be going to prison, was no more remarkable than that a labourer in working clothes should be going to work'.[3] His reference to '"gentility" hiding … its head in red nightcaps' and putting on 'heavy shoes'[4] is an indication of class roles that have been subverted by the adoption of the clothing of another class.

In fact dress is a central theme in the novel and it portrays character, status and class. Dickens makes many passing references to characters who are defined by their clothes, such as the working-class 'mender of roads' in his blue cap, 'without which he was nothing'[5] but who, by the later stages of the novel (and the Revolution), 'wore a red cap now in place of his blue one'. Then there is Jacques in his wooden shoes[6] and English Mr Lorry in his 'little wig'.[7] Clothing also disguises class as it does for the noble émigré who had fled 'in his own cook's dress'.[8] It is also central to Dickens's plot; towards its denouement, along with the swapping of clothes comes the deliberate swapping of Charles Darnay's and Sydney Carton's respective identities.[9] Perhaps most interesting are the ways in which the performative aspect of clothing and textile crafts are used to signify deeper emotional states: for example, having been unjustly incarcerated in the Bastille before the opening of the novel, Dr Manette always reverts to the shoemaking he undertook when he was first under stress, 'substituting the perplexity of the fingers for the perplexity of the brain'.[10]

Dickens pays much attention to the knitting done by the radical Madame Defarge, a direct reference to the knitting conducted alongside the radical activities of female revolutionaries known as 'Les Tricoteuses' (see later). A number of chapter headings in the novel refer to knitting: 'Knitting' and 'Still Knitting' (Book the Second, chapters 15 and 16, respectively); and chapter 14 of Book the Third (penultimate chapter of the novel) is aptly entitled 'The Knitting Done', in which Madame Defarge meets her end. On one level the knitting is a means of keeping the mind off hunger:

> All the women knitted. They knitted worthless things; but the mechanical work was a mechanical substitute for eating and drinking; the hands moved for the jaws and the digestive apparatus: if the bony fingers had been still, the stomachs would have been more famine-pinched.[11]

Furthermore, Madame Defarge's knitting becomes a kind of metaphorical shorthand for her radical activities and her particular talent for observation and visual recall. 'It would be easier', says Dickens, 'for the weakest poltroon that lives to erase himself from existence, than to erase one letter of his name or crimes from the knitted register of Madame Defarge.'[12] While knitting is normally associated with benign domesticity, Madame Defarge, when asked what she is knitting, says she has much to do and makes 'many things', adding menacingly, 'shrouds'![13] In *A Tale of Two Cities* Dickens thus uses dress as metaphor to convey both the superficial and more covert meanings of the cultures of appearances of his time and that of the immediate past.

With the expansion of the textile and clothing industries, the poor were increasingly aspirational in terms of clothing, and this desire was fuelled as much by the demand for the material acquisition of goods as it was by the wish to emulate one's social superiors. Consumption patterns and the popularity of particular fabrics were therefore linked to their increased availability, and the technological 'revolution' that facilitated these changes will be considered in Chapter 3. However, an alternative – though not necessarily conflicting – interpretation is that what was in fact emerging was a cult of working-class dress. This implied a rejection of fashion as it had been defined prior to the eighteenth century and as monopolised by the ruling and wealthy classes. The tendency that emerged in interesting ways during the last decade of the eighteenth century might today be described as 'anti-fashion'. Indeed, in the months leading up to the Reign of Terror (1793–4) in France, the very concept of (aristocratic) fashion was under attack.

It is no coincidence then that the advent of the emergence of class itself was both causative and symptomatic of the dissolution of clothing consumption patterns hitherto determined by inherited or acquired rank. Fashion would eventually become democratised, the first step in this direction symbolised by the loosening of the restrictions on the consumption of fabric and clothing that had been imposed by sumptuary legislation.

Sumptuary legislation

Historically, sumptuary laws established the means by which fabric and clothing could lever social and economic control by, for example, supporting national trade against foreign competition. They were also a way of conferring elite status. Over the three-hundred-year period from the mid-fourteenth to the early seventeenth century there were in total nine major statutes relating to apparel in England. In 1337 all but the most elevated ranks were prohibited from wearing fur and foreign apparel with other statutes following in 1363, 1463, 1483, 1510, 1515 (there were two in this year), 1533 and 1554. The last of these remained in force until 1604.[14] It is often assumed that they were enacted first and foremost to prevent people from 'dressing above their station'.[15] While this is a contributory explanation, it is also an oversimplification.

Although the primary justification in England for the regulation of dress was economic in the attempt to ensure that wealth did not leave the country in exchange for foreign textiles and garments, the statutes passed during the reign of Henry VIII were also intended to deter individuals from overindulging in dress beyond their means. In addition, there was a moral imperative: to guard against the sin of pride.[16] As Richard Allestree explained: 'There is … distinction of quality to be observed in apparel: God hath placed some in a higher condition than others; and in proportion to their condition, it befits their clothing to be. Gorgeous apparel, our Saviour tells us, is for King's courts'.[17] Not restricted to court etiquette, a further example of the way in which rank dictated attire in the Early Modern period was at royal funerals. Susan Vincent notes how the cloth from which garments were made was supplied by the estate of the deceased and given to the mourners on the basis of their rank according to rules laid down by the College of Arms.[18]

Significantly women were omitted from the apparel orders in England until 1574, although this was followed by their sudden inclusion, a change which may have been connected to both the politics and the person of the ruling monarch Elizabeth I.[19] But as Rebecca Arnold points out, fashion continually mutates, albeit at a slower rate during this period, so that it was hard for the legislature to keep up with these changes.[20] Most sumptuary laws were repealed by 1700 because they were ineffectual and in theory, this meant that 'for the first time, people of all classes were permitted to wear fashionable, luxurious dress, provided that they could afford it'.[21] The birth of 'modern' fashion – seasonal, international, corporate, media-driven and constantly changing – coincided with the birth of class, and that these evolved in tandem is more than mere coincidence. From the late 1780s, the turn of political events in France ignited consciousness of the many inequalities – political, social and economic – both on the continent and further afield as news of events in Paris spread to England. Fabric and clothing became powerful indicators and, significantly, symbols of class assertion, abnegation and conflict.

The silk and furs worn by royalty and nobility in the Early Modern period were significant for bestowing upon the wearer both an association with stability and permanence, as well as that distinction referred to earlier.[22] But with the disappearance of sumptuary legislation in the seventeenth century and the growing importance of alternative means of denoting distinction as in the wearing of lace and embroidery, fur lost its exclusive association with the elite. The woman in Pieter de Hooch's *A Woman Peeling Apples* (1663) wears a silk jacket edged with fur. There is no reason to suggest that this is not a depiction of reality evidencing the way in which luxury fabrics had in fact filtered down to the middling ranks and that this was how women dressed in domestic situations in homes that must have been cold and draughty. There is also an inferred value ascribed to woman's activity and to the domestic tasks they are here engaged in. Such jackets (edged with fur) are similar in style to many that appear elsewhere in de Hooch's work as well as in scenes of calm domesticity by Johannes Vermeer (1632–1675), in which women are engaged either in domestic tasks, reading letters or playing a musical instrument (Figure 2.1). In Amsterdam this type of jacket was known as a 'jak' and in Delft as a 'manteltje'. Throughout the third quarter of the seventeenth century, jakken were worn, says Marjorie Wiseman, by women at every level of society: common versions were made in sturdy fabrics and sensible dark colours while more elegant ones were in silk or plush in a rainbow of shades, both lined with, and trimmed with decorative bands of, snowy white fur. Although such jackets, similar to those seen in paintings, are regularly mentioned in inventories – the posthumous inventory of Vermeer's household effects made in 1676 lists 'a yellow satin mantle with white fur trimming' – not one actual garment has survived, probably, suggests Wiseman, because the garments wore out and any usable remnants were made into 'new' garments.[23] As well as being an indication of the relative prosperity of the Dutch middle ranks and those that they employed, they also denote symbolic *value* in relation to domesticity.[24] The cult of work and its associated clothing were emergent themes in Dutch genre scenes of the seventeenth century.

Figure 2.1 *Lady with Her Maidservant Holding a Letter,* by Johannes Vermeer (1632–1675), *ca.* 1666–7. Oil on canvas, 90.2 × 78.4 cm. Frick Collection, New York (Fine Art. Photo by VCG Wilson/Corbis Historical via Getty Images).

For centuries silk and fur were in the main the preserve of the elite. But Daniel Roche has argued that the 'invention' of linen marked the apogee of aristocratic civilisation, in which appearances were all-important. As well as its domestic household use for sheets, table covers and napkins, linen was *the* fabric for the making of shirts, bands, ruffs, nightwear and underwear.[25] It was continually 'renewed' through laundering and, once past its best, reused for nappies or 'clouts' for babies. It was also made into bandages for the injured and as 'rags' for menstrual bleeding. Not only was linen expensive to acquire, but it took time to care for, which also had implications for social status. Ruffs had to be remade at every wash: cleaned, dipped in starch, the pleats of the ruff were then shaped into 'sets' with heated metal irons called poking sticks. This could take up to five hours at every laundering. Time-consuming processes such as these constituted a 'statement of luxury, wealth and style'.[26] Held in place by pinning, assistance in donning a ruff implied the need for servants, thus reinforcing further the message to onlookers that the person wearing it had serious status. In the early eighteenth century, new clothes were the exception rather than the norm, with the less well-off wearing garments that they had either made or obtained second, third or fourth hand. Aside from furs and silk, fabrics such as wool, linen and cotton were more universally worn, but these generic terms hide great variety and their respective qualities (and cost) ranged from fine to coarse and from patterned to plain.

Fashion on the eve of the Revolution

I gave up all finery – no more sword, no more watch, no more white stockings, gilt trimmings and powder, but a simple wig and a good solid coat of broadcloth.

Thus it is that the substance of the poor always goes to enrich the wealthy.

Jean-Jacques Rousseau, *Reveries of the Solitary Walker*[27]

The hierarchy of social structures that demanded corresponding codes of dress and that had dominated France and much of Europe for centuries was shattered by the first years of the Revolution, from the storming of the Bastille in July 1789 to the overthrow of Robespierre and end of the Reign of Terror in July 1794. During this five-year period dress was to play such a significant role in the identification of political allegiance and the dynamics of social change that, despite both the counter-revolutionary backlash and the rebuilding of, for example, the French silk trade under Napoleon, the *ancien régime* disappeared forever, and with it, the age-old identification of the dominating determinants of fashion: elite status and wealth. Although the transition was neither even nor steady, fashion became subject to a different dynamic: working status and the cult of being poor. Although the period of the Directory (1794–9), followed by Napoleon's coup d'état of 18 Brumaire and the Empire, may be said to have reversed some of the changes brought about by the Revolution, other things had changed irrevocably. The Revolution, observes Roche, registered the triumph of the principle of diversity over that of hierarchy: 'There was no longer any way of distinguishing the classes by their clothes.'[28] But qualifying this grand statement, Roche then goes on to argue that the Revolution did not so much transform practices as accelerate certain changes. Traditional centres of influence, the court and foreign models gave way before 'philosophic and patriotic imperatives'. Shapes did not change (this, however, is, as we shall see, open to debate), but details, accessories and ways of wearing clothes quickly responded to the new order. The nation's clothes were purged of costly ornament, while 'luxury went out, but was now within reach of all citizens, since it resides in the comfort, propriety and elegance of forms'.[29] In other words, the very definition of 'luxury' was reshaped.

This powerful mood of change was fuelled by the influential ideas of the *philosophes*, and in particular by those of Jean-Jacques Rousseau (1712–1778) whose *Du Contrat Social* (*The Social Contract*) was known to have been read by Robespierre, architect of the Terror. It has often been interpreted as a blueprint for revolution. But Rousseau's views on *clothing* are of particular interest here. Like the existing political and educational systems, both of which needed reform, a clothing system dictated by wealth and rank was for Rousseau nothing less than an 'abuse': 'Fancy', he said, 'dictates [clothing], pride rules; it serves to distinguish wealth and rank. It is an abuse which cries out for reform; it would accord with the spirit of the regeneration of France to return costume to its original purpose and to egalitarian ways.'[30] The dual impact of political and technological revolution was to challenge the basis on which rank and status as both defined and represented by dress could be justified.

By the eve of the French Revolution, Paris was a major source of European fashion inspiration and influence: this may help to explain why dress itself became such a key issue during and following the events of 1789 and perhaps why the geographical reach of changes in fashion brought about by political turmoil went far beyond France. In communicating fashion news, the evolution of high-quality fashion magazines in the 1780s was of significance and proved to be a contributory factor in transmitting the volatility of ideas during the turbulent days of the Revolution. These were quick to respond to, and influence, changing fashions, a mirror of political and social events. Art was also brought into play as a powerful ideological tool, for example, the great panorama of the *Oath of the Tennis Court* (1791) by Jacques-Louis David (1748–1825) 'recorded' an event that had taken place in the early days of the Revolution, reflecting, but also influencing, the pace of political change (Figure 2.2). David's sketch some two years later of Queen Marie Antoinette on the way to the guillotine in October 1793 is a powerful portrayal of the demise of aristocracy and of the way in which the person of the queen is stripped of her finery, so that at the same time, aristocratic privilege is thereby eroded. Very much a political chameleon, David went on to exalt the heroes and martyrs of the Revolution: for example, Marat in his bath, dead at the hands of Charlotte Corday (*The Death of Marat*, 1793), who held him responsible for the September Massacres. David also designed the great revolutionary fêtes ordered by the government as well as a range of civil and official costume for a new republican world, all of these strongly influenced by classical styles. For

Figure 2.2 *Oath of the Tennis Court*, by Jacques-Louis David (1748–1825), *ca.* 1791. Drawing. Château De Versailles, Versailles (DEA/G. DAGLI ORTI. Photo by DeAgostini/Getty Images).

him, dress was a powerful form of visual communication that carried profound meaning especially during times of turbulent change.

The immediate impact of the Revolution on fashion is better illuminated by a brief discussion of fashionable styles in the period leading up to 1789. For women, the mantua gown (introduced in the 1680s) was worn widely by high- and middle-ranking women. This was a simple T-shaped dress inspired by Middle-Eastern attire, opening down the front and with a coordinating petticoat/underskirt and a separate triangular piece of fabric called the stomacher. Hooped petticoats were worn underneath to give a broad silhouette: initially, these were sturdy, linen petticoats stiffened with three or more graduated hoops of baleen (whalebone) and were introduced in the early eighteenth century in both England and France. They were cooler and probably more comfortable to wear than many layers of petticoats. For informal dress, high-ranking women adopted the 'robe à la française' or sack-back gown, so called because it fell loose at the back from a set of double box-pleats at the base of the neck (Figure 2.3). Linen undergarments kept the outer gown clean from perspiration and protected the body: women wore long chemises or shifts.

First appearing in about 1776, the 'polonaise' was an ankle-length dress with internal tapes that allowed the wearer to draw the skirt up into three distinct sections (Figure 2.4). In addition, masquerade dress and the adoption of informal styles from the Middle and Far East were reflected in the fluid lines, soft drapery and crossover styles that prepared the way for the more body-conscious fashions of the early to mid-1790s. In the latter half of the eighteenth century, *marchandes des modes*, similar in some respects to modern-day fashion designers (but distinct from milliners), became increasingly important. They were expert in designing the fashion 'confections' in both female dress and headgear that were so much a feature of the time. Perhaps the best known was Rose Bertin, whose most famous client was Queen Marie Antoinette (Figure 2.5).

Men, meanwhile, wore T-shaped linen shirts with long tails under their outer garments. Over these shirts they generally wore a three-piece suit (a Persian style that had been adopted by Charles II in 1666) consisting of collarless coat, waistcoat and breeches (Figure 2.6). The ubiquity and uniformity of the three-piece suit (worn also by labouring men) in the eighteenth century, Marcia

Figure 2.3 'Robe volante' of silk, French, *ca.* 1730. Accession no. 2010.148. Courtesy of the Metropolitan Museum of Art, New York, www.metmuseum.org (Purchase, Friends of The Costume Institute Gifts, 2010).

Pointon observes, 'rendered refinements of colour, cloth and cut of major significance as indicators of class and prestige'.[31] Silk stockings and shoes, often with costly buckles, completed the ensemble. The dominant eighteenth-century Rococo style in design was distinguished in fashion by the liberal use of trimmings and accessories, including lace ruffles, collars and tippets, and was sometimes reflected in quasi-imitation of peasant dress. For men, accessories were essential: these included hats, cravats, jewelled buttons and knee buckles. Christopher Breward argues that accessories such as stockings and buttons were particularly important in distinguishing between elite and middling styles.[32] Powdered hair and wigs were commonly worn by both men and women. In the light of this, Rousseau's pronouncement (cited at the

Figure 2.4 'Polonaise' gown of silk, French, *ca.* 1778–80. Accession no. C.I.60.40.3. Courtesy of the Metropolitan Museum of Art, New York, www.metmuseum.org (Purchase, Irene Lewisohn Bequest, 1960).

start of this section) describing his own style therefore shows him to have set himself against prevailing fashionable trends.

Children of both sexes wore ankle-length gowns of fabrics that alternated depending on the time of year but which included muslin and chintz as these fabrics became more readily available. At about the age of five, boys were breeched and subsequently clothed in garments similar to those worn by adult males.

Figure 2.5 *Queen Marie Antoinette and Her Children*, by Elisabeth-Louise Vigée-Le Brun (1755–1842), 1787. Oil on canvas, 275 × 215 cm. Musée National du Château de Versailles (Hulton Fine Art Collection. Photo by Imagno/Getty Images).

Although the political turmoil from the 1780s undoubtedly had a far-reaching impact on fashionable dress styles, changes were already taking place from at least the 1770s, which saw a relaxation of some of the very formal styles of the *ancien régime*. For example, even before the Revolution the influence of

Figure 2.6 Suit of silk, French, *ca.* 1775–80. Accession no. C.I.60.22. Courtesy of the Metropolitan Museum of Art, New York, www.metmuseum.org (Gift of International Business Machines Corporation, 1960).

the American War of Independence of 1776 'filled Paris with hairstyles à la Philadelphie and gowns of gris Americain' (the latter a reference to the colour of Benjamin Franklin's hair). 'More significantly', argues Kimberley Chrisman-Campbell, 'it got people talking about freedom and democracy, and a general trend towards egalitarianism in dress in the 1780s reflected those sentiments.[33] Hoops, wigs and hair-powder virtually disappeared from fashionable circles at this time. The influence of American democracy continued into the French revolutionary period: highly responsive to, and reflective of, political events in the fashions it featured, the fashion magazine *Le Journal de la Mode et du Goût* (June 1791) featured a bonnet 'à l'américaine'.[34]

A further influence on elite French dress from the late eighteenth century was English styles. In 1790, just after the outbreak of revolution in France, the creator of the *Journal de la Mode et du Goût*, Monsieur Le Brun, wrote that 'depuis longtemps les modes d'Angleterre font partie de celles de France' (English fashions have for a long time been part of those of France).[35] In contrast to the formal and cumbersome 'robe à la française', the fashionable 'robe à l'anglaise' (a gown with a form-fitting bodice) was adopted more widely in England. The taste for the outdoors and for physical activity produced a distinctive wardrobe among the English elite of functional, comfortable garments. Many of these garments actually originated as rural dress. The latter included hats, aprons, gaiters and frock-coats, such casual fashions being worn in England by both the landed gentry as well as the peasants who worked the estates, in contrast to the French tradition of strict social hierarchy combined with formality and luxury.[36] However, the social divisions reflected in dress in England in the last quarter of the eighteenth century were less obvious than those in France. Some styles that became increasingly popular in England from the 1760s, such as the caraco jacket (little jackets made of silk and sometimes of printed cotton) worn with a skirt, were likely to have been derived from working, 'bedgown' jackets.

The English male frock-coat (with its close fit and turned-down collar) was an important influence on European fashion, and for women the redingote (in England this was called a great coat dress) was not only practical for riding but increasingly worn as an all-purpose casual dress. In the *Journal de la Mode et du Goût* casual sporting dress is worn by a man whose style is described as 'anglo-allemant', who has the air of 'someone descending a horse or ready to mount one'! He wears coat, waistcoat and breeches and boots 'à l'anglaise'.[37] Émigrés who fled to England during the Revolution continued to wear English-inspired clothing on their return to France, thus perpetuating more relaxed and casual fashions in their native country.

English dress was equated with sober elegance and perceived to be widely divergent from the frivolity and extravagance of Parisian fashion on the eve of the Revolution. That the French emulation of English styles was purely an aesthetic choice is unlikely: there was also a link between dress and political preference, that is, the idea that a more casual mode of dress went hand in hand with a more liberal political regime and constitutional monarchy. That clothing should become symbolic of a particular political stance reveals the power of appearance and of the ways in which the cut, colour and constituents of cloth carried perception and performance beyond the material. It is this association as much as the changes themselves that are of significance in a discussion of the relation between fashion and class.

The impact of the French (sartorial) Revolution

Even from the early days of unrest in Paris, dress became a political issue. In April 1789, the Marquis de Brézé sent out instructions regarding the dress to be worn by the deputies of the three estates to the first meeting of the States General since 1614. In doing so, little did Louis XVI know, persuaded by an aristocracy that was anxious about the king's reforming ministers, the chain of events he was unleashing. In contrast to the rich clothing of the First and Second Estates (the clergy and the nobility respectively), the deputy to the Third Estate wore sombre and relatively simple costume, and it was this understated appearance that would become representative of the majority of the French population, and, subsequently, one of the most poignant symbols indicative of the early principles and rallying cries of Liberty, Equality and Fraternity. It was also the most acceptable style of dress during the Terror. Aileen Ribeiro describes the 'rules' laid down by the Marquis de Brézé as 'sartorial apartheid', arguing that they caused great offence 'because it was held to be an affront to the dignity of those who represented the majority of the people of France'.[38] The most vociferous protests against the dress regulations were those of the Comte de Mirabeau, and consequently, on 15 October 1789, they were abolished. Jacques-Louis David depicted middle-class deputies of the Third Estate in his painting of the *Oath of the Tennis Court* in the favoured costume of plain English-style cloth suits and greatcoats. In the *Journal de la*

Mode et du Goût a man is dressed in a black cloth coat ('un habit de drap noir à la Révolution'), red casimir waistcoat and yellow (they could also be black) breeches.[39] Deputies to the Third Estate were understandably resentful of the fact that their clothing was being dictated to them.

Fashion magazines chronicled the early events of the Revolution in the accessories (e.g. shoe buckles and hats) depicted: perhaps most strikingly, following the storming of the Bastille on 14 July 1789, fashion plates in the *Magasins des Modes* later in December showed two 'boucles à la Nation' and 'bonnets à la Bastille' (the latter shaped like a tower and trimmed with the tricolour ribbon). From early 1790, however, the *Journal de la Mode et du Goût* chronicled in detail important events through the clothing illustrated on its pages. One of the most tangible signs of support for the revolutionary cause was the adoption of the tricolour cockade. Symbolising the unity of the three estates, the tricolour cockade appeared shortly after 14 July 1789 and was widespread by that autumn: white was the colour of the Bourbons; red and blue those of the people of Paris. The tricolour cockade became compulsory for men in July 1792 and for women in September 1793.

As the Revolution turned into civil war between those who were 'for' or 'against' the Revolution (France would later muster its actual military forces in preparation for war), military-type clothing appeared in the pages of the *Journal de la Mode et du Goût* worn by a 'femme patriote avec le nouvel uniforme'.[40] Perhaps most interesting is a 'costume à l'égalité' in which a woman wears a 'bonnet' ('très à la mode parmi les Républicains'), kerchief, pierrot jacket and skirt of printed cotton.[41] This is possibly the closest one comes in a fashion magazine of the time to the style adopted by working women. The outfit heralded a new era in its air of simplicity. Significantly this was one of the last plates of this journal published prior to the execution of Louis XVI in January 1793, the declaration of war on Britain and the establishment of the Committee of Public Safety heralding the Reign of Terror (April 1793–July 1794) during which time fashion magazines ceased publication. It is at this point that the image of the *sans culottes* (men in carmagnole jackets and loose-fitting trousers or 'pantalons' and both men and women in clogs or 'sabots') came to symbolise the emergent cult of working-class dress.

The French Revolution did not start a revolution in the way people dressed, but it accelerated and accentuated changes that were already under way.[42] Valerie Steele argues that the trend towards plainer clothes had already begun before the occurrence of the French Revolution.[43] But in the process the dress of workers, of the poor, of the 'common people', was transformed, from constituting, first and foremost, items of functional practicality associated with immediate, everyday experience, to acquiring political and philosophical significance in the wider context of the social life of the French nation. The term *sans culottes* utilised the negation of an item of dress (i.e. *without* the knee-length breeches adopted by the aristocrats and bourgeoisie and in favour of the loose-fitting, utilitarian long trousers or 'pantalons') to describe a whole class of formerly politically dispossessed people: manual labourers and the urban poor. As Roche observes, the Revolution established trousers as the symbolic garment of the *sans culottes* of 1793 although it is something of a mystery that, possibly sold or buried, they are rarely found in surviving inventories (Figure 2.7). From pictorial sources it would appear that breeches finally ceased to be worn in the 1820s, other than at official ceremonies.[44] But it is the symbolism of the references to clothing that became so powerful, linking fashion and class inextricably. Maximilien de Robespierre, meanwhile, calling himself the leader of the *sans culottes*, never, however, adopted the costume of his 'band'. Depicted by the artist Louis-Léopold Boilly in silk coat with cravat, light nankeen breeches fastened with buckles, stockings and buckled shoes and lightly powdered wig, his appearance is elegant, although this style is not to be confused with luxury, unless it be the 'new luxury' described by Roche.

The evolution of late-eighteenth-century neoclassicism – associated as it was with a new political and architectural landscape – is reflected in the art of Jacques-Louis David, and seen most powerfully perhaps in his famous *Oath of the Horatii* (1784), but the neoclassical past also became the inspiration for dress and hairstyles, giving a new radicalism to appearances that replaced Rococo frivolity and luxury. White muslin gowns and sober black suits were considered sufficiently democratic for much of the 1790s, whereas silk, unnecessary accessories, lace and trimmings were most definitely *not*. Perhaps the best-known popular fashion was the symbolic red cap of liberty, the 'bonnet rouge'. Probably first appearing in the provincial festivals of 1790 as a neoclassical allusion to the status of freed, Roman slaves, it then caught on rapidly among ordinary people (though not among women). Yet, famous

Figure 2.7 *The Singer Chenard Wearing the Costume of a* sans culotte *Standard-Bearer*, by Louis Léopold Boilly (1761–1845), 1792. Oil on panel, 33.5 × 22.5 cm. Musée de la Ville de Paris, Musée Carnavelet (photo by ullstein bild/ullstein bild via Getty Images).

as it is, it is actually something of an exception: a classical style accepted by, and largely confined to, the lower orders. Hairstyles underwent radical change with the appearance of short, cropped styles, such as 'à la Brutus' and 'à la Titus' (derived from the role of Titus as played by Talma in Voltaire's *Brutus* on 30 May 1791). In autumn 1790 the *Journal de la Mode et du Goût* reported that 'la coëffure des jeunes gens est devenue très simples' and that hair was now to be worn unpowdered.[45]

Figure 2.8 *Madame Récamier,* by Jacques Louis David (1748–1825), 1800. Oil on canvas, 174 × 244 cm. Musée du Louvre, Paris (photo by Josse/Leemage/Corbis Historical via Getty Images).

The obsession with the neoclassical past is reflected in the raised waist of women's clothing, which rose steadily higher in the years 1798–1802. Such styles can be seen in a new fashion magazine that first appeared in 1797, *Le Journal des Dames et des Modes*. Even a cursory look at well-known images such as David's portrait of Madame Récamier (1800) (Figure 2.8), reclining in a high-waisted, sheer muslin gown, hair short and curled and with a bandeau, compared with an image such as that of the formal 'robe à la française' in fashion magazines of the 1770s, suggests the extent to which fashions had changed radically in little more than two decades. Fashions associated with exclusivity had become distinctly unfashionable and cottons, simplicity and elegance had taken their place even among the 'elite'. In fact the concept of an elite is something of a misnomer at this time: it had become political or actual suicide to be singled out in terms of luxurious dress or lifestyle and much safer to be clothed in 'les étoffes de coton rayees' and robes 'économiques'.[46] Indeed, Aileen Ribeiro argues that 'the Revolution linked woollen materials, and washable cottons and linens – fabrics more easily available to the less well-off – with democracy; true republicans had supposedly less luxurious tastes than indolent, silk-clad aristocrats'.[47]

The granting of the vote to men over the age of twenty-five who paid tax altered the balance of political power in France and was mirrored in the sartorial cult of working-class clothing: cottons and linsey wolsey for women and dark cloth (not silk) for men, simpler styles and the trend towards trousers rather than breeches for men. Luxury almost disappeared: by September 1793 there were fixed maximum prices on everyday working-class fabrics and items of clothing such as linen, wools and clogs ('les sabots'). Redingotes were widely worn, making them seem the most classless of male garments. As a consequence, according to E. and J. Goncourt in their *Histoire de la Société Française pendant la Revolution* (Paris, 1854) shop sellers complained of the demise of luxurious fabrics such as those using gold and silver. M. Le Brun's claim in September 1790 that 'not for more than ten years have taffetas been as much à la mode as today'[48] was probably less a reflection of the true state of fashion affairs than a desperate plea for the fashion industry to get back on its feet. While silks and satins continued to be worn during the winter and although cotton, gauze, linen and muslin were popular during the summer, cotton was to triumph in the longer term.

Much has been made of the economic impact of the collapse of luxury textile-related industries during the Revolution, for example, the crisis in the feather trade during the Terror following emigration of part of the Parisian nobility and the temporary triumph of simplicity in dress.[49] Fashion merchants such as Madame Eloffe (who sold articles used for trimming gowns, as well as head-dresses, fichus and feathers) were adversely affected. After 1789 she was unable to sell court gowns, but instead sold cockades by the gross to her aristocratic customers. The Revolution also brought to an abrupt halt the rapid increase in luxury consumption associated with the festivities and ceremonies of Versailles.[50]

Rose Bertin sent the queen a last bill for 40,000 livres three days before 10 August 1792. The latter date marked the culmination of the attack on aristocratic fashion, when the Tuileries was sacked and the royal wardrobe ransacked and shared out by the people of Paris among themselves.[51] Significantly, Marie Antoinette was depicted wearing a simple white muslin gown on her way to her execution, a far cry from the sumptuous fabrics she wore some years earlier

Figure 2.9 *Marie Antoinette Being Taken to Her Execution on 16 October 1793*, by William Hamilton (1751–1801), 1794. Oil on canvas, 152 × 197 cm. Musée de la Révolution Française, Vizille (Hulton Fine Art Collection. Photo by Fine Art Images/ Heritage Images/Getty Images).

(Figure 2.9). Following his coup d'état, which put an end to the Directorate, Napoleon Bonaparte began measures to revive the French silk industry and reinstituted to some extent the cult of luxury among those who could afford it. In Honoré de Balzac's novel, *Old Goriot* (published 1834–5 but set in the years 1819–20) the impoverished law student Eugène de Rastignac borrows money from his family to buy clothes appropriate to the social position to which he aspires in order to launch himself into Parisian society:

> When he had tried on his evening dress, he put on his new daytime outfit, which completely transformed him. 'I am certainly as good as Monsieur de Trailes', he said to himself. 'At last, I look like a gentleman.'[52]

As Balzac's reference to the power of clothing and fabric to alter perceptions about class reveals, in the decades following the French Revolution, some of the changes that had taken place in its immediate aftermath were reversed to some extent. However, the impact of the transformation in textile production and consumption as a result of technological and social change on visual representations of class is the subject of the following two chapters. The increasing adoption of cotton by all classes revealed that the democratisation of fabric and fashion was very much in train.

3

Fabric of society: technological change and fashion

In describing the industrialisation of the late eighteenth and early nineteenth centuries in England, the principal focus of much secondary literature is the social and economic transformation of society brought about by far-reaching technological changes that took place in textiles, in particular the cotton industry. Furthermore, those writers who are mostly interested in contemporary ethical issues as they relate to 'fast fashion' often begin their narrative by tracing the origins of poverty and class inequality within the international fashion industry to the particular development of the cotton industry in England during the 'Industrial Revolution'. For example, Andrew Brooks argues that the 'international circulation of cotton/cotton products became key to catalyzing the Industrial Revolution in the north of England' and that 'the history of capitalism is bound up in the progress of textile and apparel production in Europe and North America in the eighteenth and nineteenth centuries'.[1]

While it is true that the expansion of the cotton industry from the late eighteenth century had an enormous impact in the terms described here, reappraisal of the importance of technological innovation per se has raised questions about the way the latter has the capacity on its own to transform an industry and, in its turn, society. Giorgio Riello's 2013 study, *Cotton: The Fabric That Made the Modern World*, offers an alternative narrative however. While not undermining the significance of technological innovation in changing industry, society or the way in which people dress and the amount of clothing they own – the spinning machine allowed one late-eighteenth-century European woman to produce as much yarn as three hundred women in India[2] – Riello rather considers it in context and as one part of a complex story, the other factors being changes in customer demand and the development of international networks of trade over many centuries, affecting the supply (import) of raw cotton to

England as well as the export of finished cotton products. Riello integrates the economic value of cotton within a 'larger palette', something that he hopes 'approximates a (real) world in which the economic, the cultural, the social are never separated or mutually exclusive'.[3] Riello's work also builds on Beverly Lemire's groundbreaking research on the cotton industry, which focuses on the rising demand for cotton products by all classes, especially the labouring classes, as the key to the development of the British cotton industry from the seventeenth century onwards.[4]

There is a paradox buried within this history: while, on the one hand, cotton has contributed to the phenomenal economic growth of the world in the past one thousand years – and, as far as this study is concerned, it has shaped our understanding of what has been termed the democratisation of fashion and the ability of all classes to afford (cotton) clothing – on the other hand, it is also partly to blame for the intensification of inequality. This chapter will begin with a discussion of the economic and social context for the momentous changes within, and expansion of, the cotton industry from the late eighteenth century which made possible the production and purchase of cotton fabric by consumers from different classes and on a scale that had not been possible before. This process will be considered in relation to the ways in which such changes in textiles for clothing helped bring about class change. Then the latter part of this chapter, together with Chapter 4, constitutes an exploration of how dress and fashion in relation to social class reflected social and economic transition through the lenses of selected novelists of the period, writing from the late eighteenth through to the middle of the nineteenth centuries – from Fanny Burney and Jane Austen, to Elizabeth Gaskell and Charles Kingsley, and, finally, George Eliot, Wilkie Collins and Anthony Trollope. Later, from the mid-nineteenth century, the rapid development of the ready-to-wear clothing system and changes in retailing also contributed to the process of democratisation, and this is the focus of Chapter 5.

The transformation of the cotton industry

Scholars have suggested that cotton originated in India and was first cultivated in the Indus Valley in 3200 BCE. Cotton cultivation reached both sub-Saharan Africa and southern Europe around the tenth century.[5] Before the mechanisation of the eighteenth century, the transformation of cotton from crop to finished cloth was a relatively simple process from the technological point of view.[6] Written sources indicate that the spinning wheel was known in the Middle East around 1260, that it appeared in northern India in the mid-thirteenth/early fourteenth century and that it probably came from West Asia.[7] India excelled in cotton production mainly because of its expertise in finishing (printing and painting).[8]

Around 1200, small quantities of cotton were imported from Venice to England, and from the second decade of the sixteenth century, cotton was imported directly from the Levant to Britain to be used for quilting, stuffing and yarn for candlewicks. In the late sixteenth century, the production of cotton goods was first documented in the British Isles and by the mid-seventeenth century Lancashire was an important fustian-producing region, manufacturing the majority of the 40,000 pieces of fustians (cotton and linen mixes) produced in England every year, mostly by using raw cotton imported from Smyrna and Cyprus.[9]

The period *ca.* 1500–1750 saw the emergence of a cotton industry in Europe, an industry, argues Riello, that was 'both contingent and less revolutionary than the many histories of industrialisation in the West have suggested'. A complex triangular trade network developed between Britain and Europe, Africa and America that facilitated and fostered the growing industry. The latter relied on the exchange of slaves from Africa for cloth produced in Europe and, in turn, the exchange of raw cotton (imported into England) from America for slaves to work on the cotton plantations[10] (Figure 3.1).

The emergent British cotton industry owed its development to the trade in cottons with India. In particular, knowledge of Asian printing techniques and of the specific tastes of domestic and foreign customers was crucial to the nurturing of a domestic industry. For example, British consumers preferred their Indian cottons to be printed in coloured dyes on white backgrounds as opposed to the red or deep blue backgrounds that had been the staple for consumption in South East Asia and the Near East. A technique based on waxing large parts of the fabric so that it remained undyed was expensive; however, in the last quarter of the seventeenth century European printers learned the Indian techniques of waxing and tepid indigo fermentation and by the early

Figure 3.1 Cotton picking: a white landowner overseeing black cotton pickers at work on a plantation in the southern United States, *ca.* 1875 (photo by Hulton Archive/Getty Images).

eighteenth century were experimenting with techniques unknown in Asia, the most important of which was the use of cold vats obtained by dissolving indigo in iron sulfate that allowed the printing of blue on a white background.[11] Daniel Roche has shown that on the eve of the French Revolution, 40 per cent of Parisian wage earners' wardrobes included cottons and fustians[12] but as we have seen, 'the full triumph of cotton had to wait for the end of the *ancien régime* and the mechanisation of its production'[13] (Figure 3.2).

For most of the seventeenth and eighteenth centuries, the English East India Company (EEIC) traded more than fifty varieties of cloth, although after the 1690s they began to focus on a smaller range, including baftas, chintzes, cossaes, gurras, Guinea cloth, longcloth, romalls, sallamporees, and these constituted one-half to five-sixths of imported textiles.[14] But the EEIC's disastrous speculation in 1682 of importing from their Madras factories 200,000 ready-made cotton shirts and shifts at a time when English markets were dominated by English (linen) shirts – equivalent to one garment for every two adults in London – is indicative of the fact that 'consumers were

Figure 3.2 Cotton dress ('robe à la française'), French, 1760s. Accession no. C.I.64.32.3. Courtesy of the Metropolitan Museum of Art, New York, www.metmuseum.org (Irene Lewisohn Bequest, 1964).

not yet ready to embrace cotton as a substitute for linen'. And even when the company tried to sell off the shirts and shifts at reduced prices, most of the stock remained unsold.[15]

In England, an act of 1721 – following a partial ban in 1702 – banned totally the sale and use of all Indian cottons with the exception of muslins and blue-dyed calicoes.[16] (Britain's American colonies were exempt from the ban and thus enjoyed imports of Indian cotton throughout the eighteenth century, while in France they had been prohibited in 1686, although they were frequently smuggled into the country illegally.) By the 1780s, Britain had relaxed its ban and France was importing muslin from its colonies in the West Indies. Britain had in fact developed a thriving domestic cotton industry partly as a result of the ban (which, ironically, had been intended as a measure

Figure 3.3 Cotton textile sample book, Samuel Greg, British (Manchester), 1784. Accession no. 1985.135. Courtesy of the Metropolitan Museum of Art, New York, www.metmuseum.org (Gift of Louis K. and Susan Pear Meisel, 1985).

to destroy the rising demand for cotton) by replacing Indian cottons with printed linens and mix cottons produced in Europe[17] (Figure 3.3). Cotton allowed fashion to flourish:

> Once reserved for the expensive silks of the élites, fashionable consumption came to spread socially thanks to the use of colourful printed cottons that mimicked the design and visual effect of silks at a price that was accessible to a much wider stratum of society; motifs that were previously embroidered or delicately woven could be reproduced *ad infinitum* through the medium of printing.[18]

Furthermore, cotton was washable and relatively inexpensive and for the first time the poorer classes could afford new coarse cotton for clothing while the upper classes enjoyed fine cotton textiles that had been laboriously block-printed and copperplate printed.[19] Therefore, in considering the changing relationships between fashion and class, it was not only different fabrics per se that defined relative class and status but the different degrees of *qualities* of those fabrics that could determine them.

Although historians have tended to describe the industrialisation and mechanisation of the cotton industry of the late eighteenth and early nineteenth centuries as a British phenomenon, these momentous changes took place only because the industry was already a 'global commodity'.[20] So while Britain (specifically England) may have been the focus of the transformation of the cotton industry, the network of markets that supported these developments was global. For example, the shift from consumption of Indian to European cloth from the 1740s and 1750s was closely linked to the expansion of the African and American markets and the demand for white Indian cloth that was finished (printed) in Europe.

On the one hand, the spinning and weaving inventions that took place first in England were aimed at increasing productivity and meeting the need to clothe an increasing population. The following inventions that have been so eulogised in the historiography relating to this period are normally given credit for the huge increase in productivity of cotton: John Kay's flying shuttle (1733); John Wyatt and Lewis Paul's roller spinning machine (1738); James Hargreaves' spinning jenny (1765; patented 1770); Richard Arkwright's water frame (1767; patented 1769); Samuel Crompton's spinning mule (1779); and Edmund Cartwright's power loom (1785). In 1770 the export of English-produced cottons (£200,000) was 4 per cent that of woollen textiles (£5 million), but by 1802 cotton exports actually surpassed those of woollens. Furthermore, in the period 1780–1830, the production cost of a yard of calico fell by 83 per cent and that of a yard of muslin by 76 per cent.[21]

On the other hand, the challenge prior to the 1770s was to improve the *quality* of cotton produced, specifically so that pure cotton cloth (cotton yarn for both warp and weft) could be produced rather than a mixture of cotton and linen (fustian), in which the warp was linen, which provided the requisite strength. Interestingly, rather than machinery leading to poorer quality – the two things often associated with each other in critiques of technological innovation of this period – the reverse was actually true and technological innovation in this case actually brought about improved quality. The raw cotton imported from the southern states of America increased by 6.6 per cent in the period 1800–60 while its price fell by 0.5 per cent per annum during the same period.[22] Significantly, the cotton staple from America was of the longer variety that allowed the application of new machinery (the water frame for spinning and the power loom for weaving).

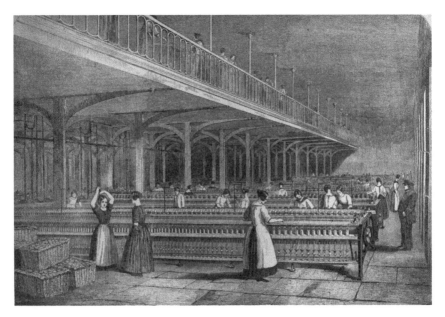

Figure 3.4 Doubling room: women doubling thread to make lace at a mill in Lancashire, England. Original Publication: *Illustrated London News*, 25 November 1851 (photo by Hulton Archive/Illustrated London News/Getty Images).

As the cotton mills came to be situated less often in the countryside – where they had been reliant on a constant source of water to power the machinery – and more and more in urban centres, they began to create their own populations due to the need for labour. The 1851 census revealed that the urban population of England was, for the first time, more numerous than the rural population; at the same time, communications (railways and roads) were improved, also leading to a degree of class levelling. Not only were different classes brought together as a result, but new retailing practices developed that could disseminate both *ideas* about the latest fashions as well as the clothing itself. The bringing together of different classes in the industrial factory setting could create class antagonism but also, eventually, a degree of class levelling in terms of wider working-class knowledge of, and access to, fashion. But up until at least the mid-nineteenth century, the story that is frequently told in fictional literature of the period is one of antagonism and difference between classes, especially between employers and the employed (Chapter 4). These antagonisms are often communicated to the reader in relation, and with reference, to dress (Figure 3.4).

Rank, manners and fashion in the English novel, 1770–1820: Fanny Burney and Jane Austen

A close reading of the novels of this period sheds light on the way clothing and fabric contributed to definitions of rank during this time and the manner in which emerging perceptions of class along with 'appropriate' ways of dressing divided – but also brought together – different groups of people. The last decades of the eighteenth century were a period of momentous change, not just in terms of the transformation of the cotton industry described earlier, but also as reflected in the evolving styles of fashionable dress. These have already been considered in part as a result of political upheaval in France during the Revolution and the ideals of equality that were reflected in a rejection of expensive silks and an 'artificial' silhouette produced by the tightly laced stays and numerous layers of fabric of mid-eighteenth-century female styles. The adoption of simpler and classically inspired outlines lent themselves to the new cotton fabrics, especially muslin, that could be obtained more readily and be more easily afforded by a larger proportion of the population by the end of the eighteenth century and into the early nineteenth century. It is true that from the second decade of the nineteenth century, the female silhouette changed again and the waist began once more to be increasingly restricted using corsets while skirts became wider and more voluminous with the aid of layers of petticoats and, eventually around mid-century, the crinoline. However, cotton was very much here to stay.

It is significant that these changes came about when the novel was establishing itself as a new art form. In the novels of both Fanny Burney (1752–1840) and Jane Austen (1775–1817) the action often takes place against a background in which the values of one rank or class are frequently pitched against those of the other; what is actually happening is that one class is trying – mostly unsuccessfully in the author's view – to imitate and adopt the values of the one above them. However, the latter usually retaliates by aiming to demonstrate that they are superior to the 'vulgarity' of the lower or lower middle classes who attempt to raise themselves in society and display their new-found status, frequently through their clothing. To this end, Fanny Burney uses irony and humour in describing the story of her beautiful heroine Evelina, writing scathingly of those so obviously lower in status than her in her successful novel of that name (1778).

Although brought up by her guardian the Rev. Mr Villars who, we are left in no doubt, is a true 'gentleman', Evelina's ignominious background (disowned by her father and orphaned by the death of her mother) places her in a position from which, over the course of the novel, she moves between two worlds; the first is that of her guardian, and the Mirvan family and Lady Howard. Here delicacy of feeling, politeness and discretion are the hallmarks of respectability, and these values are contrasted with the world of her grandmother Madame Duval and her cousins the Branghtons, in whose lives brashness and a lack of propriety and taste when it comes to manners and personal appearance are the order of the day. Written as a series of letters between the principal characters, the novel gives some fascinating insights into the material world of 1770s England and, in particular, the clothing acquired and worn by the wealthy and aspiring middle classes. Fanny Burney gives the reader a detailed account of shopping in London; she describes, for example, visits to the mercers for silk to be made up into gowns and also for caps and gauzes.[23] Evelina describes how, having chosen the fabric, 'the dispatch with which they work in these great shops is amazing, for they have promised me a compleat (*sic*) suit of linen against the evening'.[24] As Penelope Byrde points out, hats and bonnets were customary wear out of doors but for married women and ladies in their late twenties onwards, caps were worn indoors: 'The making of caps and trimming of bonnets were carried on to a considerable extent at home and formed an important topic of conversation whenever dress was discussed.'[25]

The elaborate hairstyles of the period are also described. In preparation for a private ball, Evelina's hair has been fashionably dressed:

> I have just had my hair dressed. You can't think how oddly my head feels; full of powder and black pins, and a great cushion on the top of it. I believe you would hardly know me, for my face looks quite different to what it did before my hair was dressed. When I shall be able to make use of a comb for myself I cannot tell, for my hair is so much entangled, *frizled* they call it, that I fear it will be very difficult.[26]

Although accounts of the absurdities of fashion are given in an apparently serious tone by the naïve Evelina, Fanny Burney's descriptions are clearly intended to be humorous and tongue-in-cheek. For example, in a postscript to one of her letters, Evelina adds that 'poor Miss Mirvan cannot wear one of the caps she made because they dress her hair too large for them'.[27]

As the novel progresses Madame Duval is drawn as a ridiculous and pathetic character. As the epitome of poor taste, she cannot of course see the irony of her pronouncements when she deplores 'the monstrous vulgar look' of women at Ranelagh Pleasure Gardens wearing hats and asserts that 'there's no such thing to be seen in Paris'.[28] Meanwhile, in her banter with Captain Mirvan, the stereotyping of French fashions and manners becomes an ongoing theme, Madame Duvall suggesting on one occasion that it would do him good to spend time in France. The Captain replies:

> What, I suppose you'd have me learn to cut capers? – and dress like a monkey? – and palaver in French gibberish? – hay, would you? – And powder, and daub, and make myself up, like some other folks?[29]

Burney thus exploits contemporary perceptions of English gentility and sobriety in appearance in contrast to the flamboyance of Paris fashions and to us, as readers with the benefit of knowing what happened in France eleven years after the publication of the novel, this might seem to be a sober foretaste of things to come: the rejection of the frivolities of fashion by the French revolutionaries (Chapter 2).

Penelope Byrde explains that it was not considered polite to comment in public on other people's personal appearance during this period; those of Jane Austen's characters who are interested in dress and talk about it to an excessive extent are 'unfortunately those whose vacant minds or poor manners are underlined by this habit' – such as Miss Steele in *Sense and Sensibility* (1811), Lydia Bennet in *Pride and Prejudice* (1813), Mrs Elton in *Emma* (1816) and Mrs Allen in *Northanger Abbey* (published posthumously in 1817).[30] In conversation with Marianne Dashwood, Miss Steele's inquisitiveness is represented as being in very poor taste:

> Nothing escaped *her* minute observation and general curiosity; she saw everything, and asked everything; was never easy till she knew the price of every part of Marianne's dress; could have guessed the number of her gowns altogether with better judgement than Marianne herself, and was not without hopes of finding out before they parted, how much her washing cost per week, and how much she had every year to spend upon herself.[31]

This displayed interest in the detail of other people's clothes is also considered rude in Fanny Burney's world. Of the Branghtons, Evelina says (sarcastically!) that their comments about her dress are 'equally interesting and well-bred':

> The young ladies began, very freely, to examine my dress, and to interrogate me concerning it. 'This apron's your own work, I suppose, Miss? but these sprigs a'n't in fashion now. Pray, if it is not impertinent what might you give a yard for this lutestring? – Do you make your own caps, Miss? –'[32]

Burney shows how appearance defines gentility and – as it was still described at this period – rank.[33] The cost of clothing is a significant indicator of wealth and status but it is mostly seen as such by those who, according to Burney, *lack* taste and think too much about these things rather than taking them for granted, so avoiding the need to discuss them. The assumption made by Miss Branghton, that Sir Clement Willoughby's profession must be 'something very genteel … because he dresses so fine', is naïve. Worse still – and in the utmost poor taste – is the way that Mr Smith describes Sir Clement Willoughby's income in relation to his clothes: 'for I'm sure he did not get that suit of cloaths he had on, under thirty or forty pounds; for I know the price of cloaths pretty well'.[34] By contrast those who possess wealth and status do not, according to Fanny Burney, need to calculate the cost of a genteel appearance.

A further example of the role clothing and accessories play in distinguishing rank is in the discussion that takes place intermittently over several pages about the types of dress to be worn depending on where one sits at the opera, including the wearing or non-wearing of hats.[35] The men also discuss women and the wearing of rouge, implying that 'respectable' women do not wear it. Lord Orville, whose aristocratic status goes hand in hand with his role as an arbiter of good taste, describes the difference between the effect of rouge and the natural colour of a woman's (Evelina's) complexion:

> The difference of natural and artificial colour seems to me very easily discerned; that of Nature, is mottled, and varying; that of art, *set*, and *too* smooth; it wants that animation, that glow, that *indescribable something* which, even now that I see it, wholly surpasses all my powers of expression.[36]

In an amusing episode that verges on slapstick humour, Burney writes of the hilarity of the image of Madame Duval with her new Lyon silk 'negligee' wet through and 'quite spoilt' when it gets covered in mud after she has fallen over.[37] Later, the contrast between the natural beauty of Evelina and that of Madame Duval when the latter has been 'attacked' by 'robbers' is particularly striking. Of Madame Duval, Fanny Burney says:

> Her head-dress had fallen off; her linen was torn; her negligee had not a pin left in it; her petticoats she was obliged to hold on; and her shoes were perpetually slipping off. She was covered with dirt, weeds and filth, and her face was really horrible, for the pomatum and powder from her head, and the dust from the road, were quite *pasted* on her skin by her tears, which, with her *rouge*, made so frightful a mixture, that she hardly looked human.[38]

And then, as a final humiliation, she finds that she has also lost her curls of false hair![39]

Taste is frequently described by both Fanny Burney and Jane Austen as something which is innate and cannot be acquired. As Penelope Byrde points out, in the novels of Jane Austen, the wearing of white (especially muslin) – such as by Eleanor Tilney in *Northanger Abbey* – becomes a symbol of elegance, refinement and propriety.[40] The wearing of white gowns was a class statement; only those with means and leisure could really indulge in them. In *Mansfield Park* (1814), Mrs Norris commends a housekeeper who 'turned away two housemaids for wearing white gowns'.[41] The housemaids were clearly attempting to dress above their station.

Evelina expresses the view that taste is something that cannot be learnt when she describes Mr Smith disparagingly:

> In the afternoon, when he returned, it was evident that he purposed to both charm and astonish me by his appearance; he was dressed in a very showy manner, but without any taste, and the inelegant smartness of his air and deportment, his visible struggle, against education, to put on the fine gentleman, added to his frequent conscious glances at a dress to which he was but little accustomed, very effectually destroyed his aim of *figuring*, and rendered all his efforts useless.[42]

Likewise, Madame Duval at a ball in Hampstead draws attention to herself because she is dressed in a 'showy dress', inappropriate for her age and, even worse, she also uses 'an unusual quantity of *rouge*'.[43]

Among other things the novel can thus be seen as a satirical critique of those who attempt to emulate people above them in the social scale. That this is remarked upon by both Fanny Burney and Jane Austen reveals to the reader a glimpse of a dynamic society in which the social structures are not static; dress and appearance can be manipulated to define social, economic and cultural position in this changing world. While the pace of change may have been exaggerated by some economic historians, Beverly Lemire points out that although 'comments both before and during the eighteenth century suggest that the lure of fashionability infected British society … the frequency and unanimity of these remarks reaches its height in the mid- to late eighteenth century'.[44] For Lemire, the wearing of cottons 'spread out widely across the population' and this interpretation thus attributes to cotton the principal cause of the democratisation of fashionable dress in this period:

> If one can visualise changes over time, they would have included a more vibrant, kaleidoscopic flourish of colours and patterns across the spectrum of the population. The reds, purples, yellows, greens, blues, dots, diamonds, flowers, sprigs, spots, and checks startle the eye and invite the attention not only of contemporaries, but also of historians, to witness the visible transformation unfolding among the people of Britain.[45]

This perspective is endorsed by the fascinating research done by John Styles on the clothing worn by babies entering the London Foundling Hospital, the latter established by royal charter in 1739 for 'the maintenance and education of exposed and deserted young children'. When mothers left babies here, the Hospital often retained a small token as a means of identification, usually a piece of fabric. These swatches of fabric now form Britain's largest collection of everyday textiles from the eighteenth century. Among the wide variety of types of fabric in the collection, Styles shows how printed linens and cottons from the mid-eighteenth century 'incorporated key elements of the fashionable look of the far more expensive flowered silks worn by the wealthy classes'[46] and that 'what we see when we examine the printed fabrics among the Foundling textiles is a democratization of fashion'.[47]

Meanwhile, Lemire concludes that 'the presence and proliferation of fashionable, ready-to-wear clothing in the eighteenth-century context indicates the degree to which the diminution of visual social distinctions was an element of that period'.[48] Alongside the narratives from novels of the period which reveal the extent to which class changes were underway, well into the early decades of the nineteenth century, the number of etiquette books increased, reflecting the need by the middle and wealthy classes to maintain the status quo in a time of flux.

4

From north to south: class identity and dress in the English novel, 1820–60

Why, sir, forty years ago, when I was much such a strapping youngster as you,
a man expected to pull between the shafts the best part of his life, before he got
the whip in his hand. The looms went slowish, and fashions didn't alter quite
so fast: I'd a best suit that lasted me six years.

George Eliot, *The Mill on the Floss*[1]

The social tensions described satirically by Fanny Burney in the previous chapter perhaps seem superficial and slightly frivolous in comparison with those discussed by Victorian novelists. Working conditions in the early (northern) textile factories and the state of the (southern) countryside became the focus of well-known 'condition-of-England' novels such as Elizabeth Gaskell's *Mary Barton* (1848) and *North and South* (1855) and Charles Kingsley's *Yeast* (1848). While in the longer term the result of mass production and consumption of cotton textiles was to amount to a redefinition of class – as shown by fabric and the clothing into which it was made – in the shorter term, these writers recognised that class antagonism was partly the consequence of the transition to an industrialising society, and their 'solutions', unlike those of Karl Marx, were not so much political or economic ones but were often based on what they believed to be the need for the intervention of human feeling, understanding and discourse in order to overcome the great distrust between workers and their employers. The novels of Elizabeth Gaskell, Charles Kingsley, George Eliot, Anthony Trollope and finally Wilkie Collins provide some unique and penetrating insights into the ways in which fashion helped to define emerging class identities and relations in nineteenth-century England.

Elizabeth Gaskell: dress and class conflict

Elizabeth Gaskell (1810–1865) was living in Manchester as the wife of a Unitarian minister at the time of writing her 'industrial novels'. Her output in terms of short stories, novels and articles was prolific: of over forty stories and articles written in the fifteen-year period between 1850 and her death, two-thirds were published by Charles Dickens, either in *Household Words* or in its successor *All the Year Round*. Although she sympathises with the plight of her working-class characters, at the same time she was intensely conscious of class and the coded language communicated by dress and fabric. For example, in a letter to her daughter advising on a dress to be given to a servant as a gift on leaving her employment, she recommends that her daughter buy a *print* gown, but on no account one made of silk (Figure 4.1).[2] Dress plays an important role in exploring the major themes of the novels, *Mary Barton* and *North and South* in particular: it is often used to identify different classes, relationships between the rich and the poor and between the employer and the employed, as well as the cultural constructs that distinguish the northern (industrial) town from southern (rural) England. *Mary Barton* was originally entitled *John Barton* after the father of the heroine, but publishers Chapman and Hall objected to naming a book after a man who murders his employer – Harry Carson the mill owner. In her preface Elizabeth Gaskell describes her reasons for writing the novel:

> I bethought me how deep might be the romance in the lives of some of those who elbowed me daily in the busy streets of the town in which I resided. I had always felt a deep sympathy with the care-worn men, who looked as if doomed to struggle through their lives in strange alternations between work and want; tossed to and fro by circumstances, apparently in even a greater degree than other men … I saw that they were sore and irritable against the rich, the even tenor of whose seemingly happy lives appeared to increase the anguish caused by the lottery-like nature of their own.[3]

The Manchester mills provide the focal points of the action in both novels, significant because this is where the cotton fabric was being produced; on one level cotton is the salvation of the working classes because its manufacture provides jobs, but the dreadful conditions in which so many are employed

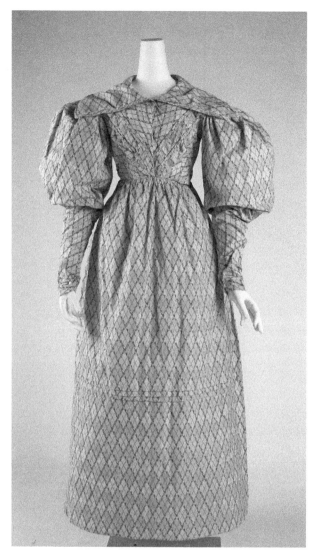

Figure 4.1 Cotton dress, British, *ca.* 1827. Accession no. 1981.12.1. Courtesy of the Metropolitan Museum of Art, New York, www.metmuseum.org (The German Fur Federation Gift, 1981).

also highlight the inequalities of the factory system as it had evolved by mid-century. As we have seen it is a fabric valued by working-class people, but Elizabeth Gaskell implies that it still separates them from the better-off: in *North and South* Mrs Hale reveals this class prejudice when she asks, 'But these factory people – who on earth wears cotton that can afford linen?'[4] In her view, linen was still the preferred choice for those who could afford it; this gives us a rather different perspective from the social and economic historical accounts encountered in the previous chapter. Meanwhile other novelists not specifically concerned with the impact of industrialisation also comment upon the relatively slow adoption of cotton by all classes.

Because the cotton industry expanded so quickly during this period and the price of the finished product was reduced, we might assume that working-class people were more likely to be able to afford it. By the mid-nineteenth century the scale of textile production had increased dramatically. As Jane Tozer and Sarah Levitt point out, 'Instead of manufacturing goods for a small, relatively prosperous section of society, the new customer was poorer, and demanded pretty fabrics which were as cheap as possible.'[5] Among the fabrics to be shown at the Great Exhibition of 1851 (catalogued in *The Journal of Designs and Manufactures*, 1849–51) were some humble prints: for example, in November 1849 a piece of purple printed calico by Thomas Hoyle and Sons of Manchester. (Hoyle's prints were very well known as serviceable fabrics.) Indeed, Elizabeth Gaskell's character Mary Barton in the novel of that name (a poor Manchester dressmaker) was described as wearing one.[6] Even so, and as already noted, much of the cotton produced was for export. So working-class people did not necessarily benefit immediately; Elizabeth Gaskell points to the way in which clothing highlighted increasing inequalities, with the rich becoming rich often at the expense of the poor. On several occasions, she represents poverty in relation to biblical narrative: in chapter 1 of *Mary Barton*, she introduces the overriding theme of the novel with reference to the well-known story of Dives and Lazarus – Dives in his 'purple and fine linen' and Lazarus in his rags. John Barton asks:

> If I am out of work for weeks in the bad times, and winter comes, with black frost, and keen east wind, and there is no coal for the grate, and no clothes for the bed, and the thin bones are seen through the ragged clothes, does the rich man share his plenty with me, as he ought to do, if his religion was not a humbug? … We are their slaves as long as we can work; we pile up their fortunes with the sweat of our brows; and yet we are to live as separate as if we were in two worlds; ay, as separate as Dives and Lazarus, with a great gulf betwixt us.[7]

Elizabeth Gaskell's reference to the well-known parable – in which Lazarus starves at the gate of the rich Dives but after death goes to be with Abraham, whereas Dives languishes in the afterlife in Hades for not sharing his riches – was intended to prick the consciences of the middle classes and to instil fear in those who believed that one's fate in an afterlife bore a direct relation to conduct in this one. As Selina Todd points out, this is a powerful use of the rich/poor dialectic, a graphic reminder that class is no romantic tradition but is produced by exploitation, in a country where a tiny elite possesses the majority of the wealth.[8]

Cotton factory worker Job Legh continues the exploitation theme when he observes with bitter irony:

> There's but hundreds of them parliament folk as wear so many shirts to their back; but there's thousands and thousands o' poor weavers as han gotten only one shirt i' th' world; ay, and don't know where t' get another when that rag's done, though they're turning out miles o' calico every day; and many a mile o't lying in warehouses, stopping up trade for want o' purchasers.[9]

The contrast of workers with 'only one shirt' to their backs with the 'parliament folk' with 'so many' is directly reminiscent of the contrast between followers of Christ who have no material wealth and those people who have much more than they need, an oblique reference to Lk. 3.11 which stipulates that those with more than one shirt should give one away to the poor. Gaskell's unequivocal message is that the rich are rich at the expense of the poor, and to illustrate this in clothing terms makes that message an extremely powerful one (Figure 4.2).

Later in the novel the point about the poverty of the factory workers is driven home when a workers' deputation arrives in the public room of a hotel for an interview with employers about wages and conditions:

> Tramp, tramp, came the heavy clogged feet up the stairs; and in a minute five wild, earnest-looking men stood in the room … Had they been larger boned men, you would have called them gaunt; as it was, they were little of stature, and their fustian clothes hung loosely upon their shrunken limbs. In choosing their delegates, too, the operatives had had more regard to their brains, and power of speech than to their wardrobes; they might have read the opinions of that worthy Professor Teufelsdruch (*sic.*) in *Sartor Resartus*, to judge from their dilapidated coats and trousers, which clothed men of

Figure 4.2 Poor home: the home of cotton mill workers in Manchester, England. Original Publication: *Illustrated London News*, November 1862 (photo by Hulton Archive/Illustrated London News/Getty Images).

parts, and of power. It was long since many of them had known the luxury of a new article of dress; and air-gaps were to be seen in their garments. Some of the masters were rather affronted at such a ragged detachment coming between the wind and their nobility; but what cared they?[10]

There is pathos here, with the descriptions of the workers' poverty tinged with irony at the suggestion that their raggedness is not a reflection of ragged brains or a lack of power of speech. The reference to fustian[11] is significant: in *The Condition of the Working Class in England in 1844* Friedrich Engels observes that 'fustian has become the proverbial costume of the working men' of the Manchester mills, 'who are called "fustian jackets", and call themselves so in contrast to the gentlemen who wear broadcloth, which latter words are characteristic of the middle classes'.[12] In George Eliot's novel *Felix Holt, the Radical* (1866), set some thirty years previously around the time of the passing of the 1832 Reform Act, the author makes the same association between the wearing of broadcloth and middle-class status: the electioneering agent John Johnson is described as a 'smartly-dressed personage on horseback, with a conspicuous expansive shirt-front and figured satin stock'. Johnson was a 'stout man, and gave a strong sense of broadcloth' and he is contrasted with the colliers, 'in their good Sunday beavers and coloured handkerchiefs serving as cravats, with the long ends floating'.[13] Johnson is later described as 'serviceable John Johnson, himself sleek, and mindful about his broadcloth and his cambric fronts'.[14]

Meanwhile, in order to identify with his working-class audience, the well-known Chartist leader Feargus O'Connor was reported to have dressed in fustian when he addressed a Chartist meeting.[15] Wearing a specific fabric in this way became a visual mark of identification with others of working-class status. It can therefore also be used as an effective disguise; for example, in *North and South* the counterfeit Leonards dresses up in fustian in order to look 'just like a working man'.[16] Nicholas Higgins, the 'drunken infidel weaver',[17] wears his 'usual fustian clothes' to Mrs Hales' funeral, but he also makes a concession to what would have been considered middle-class respectability and the etiquette of mourning by wearing a 'bit of black stuff sewn round his hat – a mark of mourning which he had never shown to his daughter Bessy's memory'.[18]

In *Mary Barton*, Jem Wilson is described as a 'black, grimy mechanic in dirty fustian clothes' and is contrasted with the middle-class mill owner Harry Carson. Judging Jem purely by his appearance, Carson cannot believe that Jem could be a serious rival for the affections of Mary, recalling his own reflection which 'he had so lately quitted in his bedroom'.[19] When Jem puts his 'black, working right hand' on Carson's arm to detain him, the latter 'shook it off, and with his glove pretended to brush away the sooty contamination that might be left upon his light greatcoat sleeve'.[20] The contrast drawn by Elizabeth Gaskell between Jem's sooty black hand and Carson's lightly coloured greatcoat becomes a metaphor for their different class status. At the end of the novel, and because there seems to be no 'solution' to the divisions between the classes, Mary and Jem Wilson emigrate even though Jem is finally acquitted of the murder charge.

At the beginning of *North and South*, middle-class Margaret Hale, as a result of a change in family circumstances, has no choice but to move from the rural south of England to the industrial northern town of Milton-Northern (based on Manchester). Elizabeth Gaskell gradually picks apart the 'myth' of the southern rural idyll; not only do we follow Margaret's gradual acceptance of the life and values of the north, but we also watch the development of her relationship with mill owner John Thornton, which moves from mutual dislike and distrust to eventual understanding and love. However, as Jenny Uglow points out, 'the combative relationship of Margaret Hale and the millowner John Thornton ... is far from an exact analogy to the class relations of industrial capitalism'.[21] The eventual marriage of John and Margaret represents the coming together of two opposite worlds – that of north and south – but the question of class divide represents a real problem for Gaskell. In the novel, there is, however, some coming together of different classes, for example, the middle-class Margaret makes friends with the young, working-class girl Bessy Higgins, who is dying of consumption as a result of working in the cotton carding room. They are united by their mutual interest in dress but the class difference manifested through their respective clothing remains for the time being: 'And now that Margaret was there, and had taken a chair by her, Bessy lay back silent, content to look at Margaret's face, and touch her articles of dress, with a childish admiration of their fineness of texture.'[22]

Later in the novel we discover that Bessy, before she died, had requested that she be buried in a garment belonging to Margaret. So even if clothing highlights class difference in life, in death it can take on a symbolic role, forging a bond to unite different interests and classes. Half a century on from the writing of Fanny Burney and Jane Austen – who, as we have seen, thought it impolite to ask too many questions about another woman's clothing – by contrast, Elizabeth Gaskell shows it to be a way of bringing women of different social positions together towards mutual feeling and trust:

> The girls, with their rough, but not unfriendly freedom, would comment on her (Margaret's) dress, even touch her shawl or gown to ascertain the exact material; nay, once or twice, she was asked simple questions relative to some article which they particularly admired. There was such a simple reliance on her womanly sympathy with their love of dress, and on her kindliness, that she gladly replied to these inquiries, as soon as she understood them; and half smiled back at their remarks.[23]

Charles Kingsley: the rural 'problem'

Like Elizabeth Gaskell, Anglican clergyman Charles Kingsley (1819–1875) was deeply concerned with the social and economic conditions endured by the poor; as well as novels, he wrote numerous sermons, lectures and pamphlets. However, he condemned revolutionary ideas, which he saw as prevalent within the Chartist movement, and instead called for reforms that would bring about social improvement. But whereas Elizabeth Gaskell's work deals in the main with the industrial north, Charles Kingsley's *Yeast* (1848) deals with the problem of unsanitary conditions and disease in the English countryside. In the mid-nineteenth century, living conditions were deplorable in many rural areas and the lives of working-class people in agriculture were uncertain with wages low and unemployment rife. *Yeast* derives its title from the author's description of the book as 'an honest sample of the questions which, good or bad, are fermenting in the minds of the young of this day, and, are rapidly leavening the minds of the rising generation.'[24] These 'questions' frequently gravitate around the 'condition' of the working classes.[25]

The plot describes the fate of Lancelot Smith, a wealthy young man, who changes his religious and social views under the influence of Paul Tregarva, a philosophical game-keeper, who acquaints Smith with the social, economic and moral conditions of the rural poor. Kingsley's conclusions about what needs to be done to address the 'condition-of the-poor' question are informed by a thorough knowledge of the parliamentary bluebooks, of which there was a proliferation in the Victorian period: thus 'Lancelot buried himself up to the eyes in the Condition-of-the-Poor-question – that is, in bluebooks, red books, sanitary reports, mine reports, factory reports.'[26] On a number of occasions it is evident that the 'opinions' expressed in the text are lifted more or less directly from these sources such as when Paul Tregarva expresses the view that fieldwork undertaken by rural women 'wears them out in body … and makes them brutes in soul and in manners.'[27] This echoes the findings of the parliamentary commissioners who, in 1843 and with various agendas, conducted their survey into the employment of women and children in agriculture. Their reports discredited the employment of women outside the home in agriculture, which, they thought, made them neglectful of their domestic 'duties' of cooking, cleaning and mending clothes.[28]

Fustian appears again in a reference to 'serfs' wearing fustian jackets.[29] The word 'serf' here is anachronistic given that rural working-class men and women who worked on the land in the mid-nineteenth century were more commonly referred to as labourers and field-women respectively. The latter were wage labourers while serf has the connotation that the worker was bound both to the soil and to their employers, though perhaps this is a deliberate use of the term by the author precisely to make this point. But more significant is that the term 'fustian jackets' became so closely linked with working-class men that, as Engels pointed out, the men were named by the garments with which they were associated, rather than just being described as *wearing* fustian jackets (discussed earlier). Kingsley also exploits the symbolic value of that other item of clothing that associated itself with working-class men in the countryside: the smock-frock (or smock). Worn as an overgarment from the late eighteenth to the late nineteenth century, smocks were made from a variety of fabrics ranging from fine linen to thicker cotton or cotton mixes. They were loose fitting and often beautifully embroidered but became increasingly obsolete as ready-made suits and other clothing became more widely available as a result of changing manufacturing and retail practices and better transport linking town with countryside, especially that facilitated by the railways from the 1840s. As agricultural practices became mechanised, smocks were also considered dangerous due to the large amount of fabric from which they were made and which was apt to catch on agricultural machinery. But prior to its going out of fashion in the last decades of the nineteenth century the smock came to be seen as virtually synonymous with rural working-class status. Thus in order to enable Lancelot Smith to conduct his research into rural 'conditions', Paul Tregarva suggests he go with him to a village revel but says that Lancelot must go dressed in a smock in order to disguise himself as a working-class labourer if he is to ascertain the information he wants: 'You are not ashamed of putting on a smock-frock? For if you go as a gentleman, you will hear no more of them than a hawk does of a covey of partridges.'[30]

There were marked differences between the north and the south not just in terms of people's perceptions, such as those described by Elizabeth Gaskell in *North and South*, but in actual terms of wages and 'access' to more – and more *fashionable* – clothing. Though not without its bias, the report following the second parliamentary commission of enquiry into the employment of women and children in agriculture (1868–9) is a useful source not least because the commissioners comment frequently on the clothing of the poor and how they acquired it. In northern counties the competition of alternative employment provided by manufacturing industries meant that agricultural labour was relatively scarce and this factor helped to drive wages up. The point is illustrated by one of the commissioners H. S. Tremenheere, who, referring to northern Lancashire, observes that the county's 'vast manufacturing development' causes a 'general scarcity of agricultural labour'.[31] The commissioners made interesting comparisons between the relative prosperity of north and south – in Cumberland and Westmorland there is said to exist a 'passion for dress' among the female farm servants:

> No inconsiderable part of the wages of a farm servant girl is expended on her person. At church it would be difficult to distinguish a farm servant from the daughter of a statesman or of a substantial tenant farmer, and a girl whose ordinary costume is a coarse petticoat, pinned close round her body, and wooden clogs, will appear at a dance in a white muslin dress, white kid boots and gloves, and with a wreath of artificial flowers on her head.[32]

We shall never know how accurate the observations of the commissioners actually were but there were clearly regional differences in people's access to fashionable clothing depending on income, occupation and stage in life. Furthermore, they point to a gradual levelling of class difference so far as it was reflected in dress.

George Eliot's 'middle England': the quest for respectability

The work of George Eliot (born Mary Ann Evans in 1819) reveals the subtle distinctions of clothing among small rural and provincial communities in the Midland counties. Albeit that she was writing under her pseudonym George Eliot, Charles Dickens guessed the author of *Scenes of Clerical Life* (1858) to be a woman, which he inferred from the 'womanly touches' and 'such marvels of description as Mrs Barton sitting up in bed to mend the children's clothes'.[33] Details of dress are also minutely observed in both *Adam Bede* (1859) and *The Mill on the Floss* (1860). *Adam Bede* shows the complexity of class in the period but in particular recalls the 1830s (the time of the author's childhood and young adulthood), highlighting the differences not only between the gentry and the working classes but also between artisans and small tenant farmers and the less 'respectable'. In both novels Eliot shows the economic vulnerability of artisans and small tenant farmers and how relatively easy it was for these groups – as a result of making unwise choices, often as a result of a 'flaw' in character – to 'fall' into the class below. In *Adam Bede*, such a fate befalls beautiful Hetty Sorrel after her seduction by Captain Donnithorne, as well as the Tulliver family in *The Mill on the Floss* after Mr Tulliver's unfortunate decision to take his case to law brings down the whole of his immediate family.

George Eliot presumably experienced some of the precariousness of the poor as, after having left school at the age of sixteen, and following the death of her mother, she kept house for her father in 1836–7. At this time she was disturbed by poverty, and feeling guilty at her own plenty, she organised a local clothing club.[34] She must have known that charity, while efficacious, was also undesirable and often only a last resort. In *Adam Bede*, she goes to great lengths to describe the 'respectable' working class. We are told that Hetty, like her aunt Mrs Poyser and the family with whom she lives, does not want to rely on charity but has 'the pride not only of a proud nature but of a proud class – the class that pays the most poor rates, and most shudders at the idea of profiting by a poor rate'.[35] Adam and Seth Bede are described as hard-working and dependable, Adam 'the stalwart workman in paper cap, leather breeches, and dark-blue worsted stockings'.[36] After the death of their father, the brothers carry his coffin in their 'rusty working clothes'.[37] Meanwhile Lisbeth (Adam and Seth's mother) and Mrs Poyser demonstrate their respectability by never being idle and always doing something with their hands, such as knitting.[38]

Indeed Mrs Poyser, like her niece Dinah Morris, could not be more different in comparison with her other niece Hetty, and such differences in character are often described in terms of divergent attitudes to clothing. For example, 'the most conspicuous article' in Mrs Poyser's attire was 'an ample checkered linen apron, which almost covered her skirt; and nothing could be plainer or less noticeable than her cap and gown, for there was no weakness of which she was less tolerant than feminine vanity, and the preference of ornament to utility'.[39] Even though Sunday was 'the day when all must be in their best clothes and their best humour',[40] Mr Poyser likewise epitomises respectability in his 'Sunday suit of drab, with a red-and-green waistcoat and a green watch-ribbon having a large cornelian seal attached ...; a silk handkerchief of a yellow tone around his neck; and excellent grey ribbed stockings, knitted by Mrs Poyser's own hand'.[41] Meanwhile the Poyser children Marty and Tommy (aged nine and seven respectively) are described as wearing 'little fustian tailed coats and knee-breeches'.[42] There is often a note of nostalgia in George Eliot's description of the styles of the past and of how clothing and fabric were obtained formerly compared with current practices. For example, she describes Mrs Poyser's tablecloth as

> a cloth made of homespun linen, with a shining checkered pattern on it, and of an agreeable whitey-brown hue, such as all sensible housewives like to see – none of your bleached 'shop-rag' that would wear into holes in no time, but good homespun that would last for two generations.[43]

Another of the themes that recurs in the novel is the contrast in the aspirations and fates of those who focus on dress and appearance – such as the beautiful Hetty – and those who concentrate their lives on serving others, like Dinah Morris, the Methodist preacher. Dinah is described at the beginning of the novel as wearing a 'black stuff dress' and 'a net Quaker cap'.[44] Meanwhile the blacksmith's daughter, Bessy Cranage, wears 'a pair of large round ear-rings with false garnets in them, ornaments condemned not only by the Methodists, but by her own cousin'; this is in contrast to the Methodists who wear 'Quakerlike costume'.[45] Dinah addresses Bessy when preaching: 'You think of ear-rings and fine gowns and caps, and you never think of the Saviour who died to save your precious soul.'[46] Of Hetty Sorrel, George Eliot says:

> It is little use for me to say how lovely was the contour of her pink-and-white neckerchief, tucked into her low plum-coloured stuff bodice, or how the linen butter-making apron, with its bib, seemed a thing to be imitated in silk by duchesses, since it fell in such charming lines, or how her brown stockings and thick-soled buckled shoes lost all that clumsiness which they must certainly have had when empty of her foot and ankle – of little use, unless you have seen a woman who affected you as Hetty affected her beholders.[47]

Hetty's seduction by Arthur Donnithorne, the young squire, is disastrous; not only does Hetty – in the eyes of both society and of herself – lose her 'reputation' and her self-respect, but it reveals the unlikely prospect of long-term relationships and marriage between different classes at this period. From the beginning Donnithorne is shown to be different from his tenants, not least in terms of the 'difference of costume', with his 'striped waistcoat, long-tailed coat, and low top-boots'.[48] Hetty's attraction to Arthur is fuelled by her assumption that it will enable her to climb the social ladder: her dreams 'were all of luxuries: to sit in a carpeted parlour, and always wear white stockings; to have some large beautiful ear-rings, such as were all the fashion; to have Nottingham lace round the top of her gown, and something to make her handkerchief smell nice, like Miss Lydia Donnithorne'.[49] After Arthur Donnithorne has kissed her she 'dresses up' before she goes to bed in the privacy of her humble bedroom and puts on some large ear-rings (made of coloured glass) and parades in front of her glass imagining being a lady.[50] Later in the novel she dresses up for Arthur's birthday feast and dreams again of being a lady.[51] If she cannot become a 'lady' then the next best thing is to be a lady's maid and to this end she gets instruction from Mrs Pomfret to learn to do 'lace-mending' and 'stocking-mending' in a way that 'you can't tell it's been mended'.[52] But these aspirations turn out to be completely unrealistic and the class system prevents Hetty from realising her ambition.

Thus dress plays an important part in maintaining and reinforcing the class system as when the prizes of clothing given out by Lydia Donnithorne at the birthday feast to humble villagers are only what are 'useful and substantial'. Lydia says: 'I should not think of encouraging a love of finery in young women of that class'.[53] As in the writing of Fanny Burney, the characters in George Eliot's novels assume that class and being a lady is 'in the blood' and that class lines cannot be breached. In *Felix Holt, the Radical*, Esther Lyon – brought up as the daughter of the Dissenting Minister the Rev. Rufus Lyon – is actually a 'born lady'.[54] Even before we know the truth of her parentage, we are given hints of her 'difference' from the class of her stepfather when she says how others are baffled by the fact that she, the daughter of a Dissenter, 'came to be so well educated and ladylike', describing Miss Jermyn (the daughter of Matthew Jermyn who is the lawyer of the landowning family, the Transomes) as 'vulgarity personified – with large feet, and the most odious scent on her handkerchief, and a bonnet that looks like "The Fashion" printed in capital letters'.[55]

Middle-class ascendancy: Anthony Trollope and Wilkie Collins

Anthony Trollope (1815–1882) offers a view of society through a different lens – that of the professional middle classes. Set in the fictional cathedral town of Barchester in the county of Barsetshire in the mid-nineteenth century, *The Warden* (1855) is the first of the Barsetshire series of novels. Again, we see the transformative power of clothing and how it creates a persona for middle-class male respectability, in this case those employed by the Church of England. Indeed, clothes contribute much to the imperious public persona of Archdeacon Dr Grantly, described – albeit slightly tongue-in-cheek – by Trollope as

> a fitting impersonation of the church militant here on earth; his shovel hat, large, new, and well-pronounced, a churchman's hat in every inch, declared the profession as plainly as does the Quaker's broad brim; his heavy eyebrow, large open eyes, and full mouth and chin expressed the solidity of his order; the broad chest, amply covered with fine cloth, told how well to do was his estate; one hand ensconced within his pocket, evinced the practical hold which our mother church keeps on her temporal possessions; and the other, loose for action, was ready to fight if need be in her defence; and below these the decorous breeches, and neat black gaiters showing so admirably that well-turned leg, betokened the decency, the outward beauty, and grace of our church establishment.[56]

The ability of clothing to create the image of power associated with Dr Grantly is only fully appreciated when we view him in his night-clothes, an ordinary man after all: ''Tis only when he has exchanged that ever-new shovel hat for a tasselled nightcap, and those shining black habiliments for his accustomed *robe de nuit*, that Dr Grantly talks, and looks, and thinks like an ordinary man.'[57]

In contrast to the worldly Dr Grantly, the Rev. Septimus Harding, around whom the novel revolves, is the unambitious elderly warden of Hiram's Hospital, a charity home established more than four hundred years earlier for a dozen labourers no longer able to earn their daily bread:

> Mr Harding is a small man, now verging on sixty years but bearing few of the signs of age; his hair is rather grizzled, though not grey, his eye is very mild, but clear and bright, though the double glasses which are held swinging from his hand, unless when fixed upon his nose, show that time has told upon his sight: his hands are delicately white, and both hands and feet are small; he always wears a black frock-coat, black knee-breeches, and black gaiters, and somewhat scandalizes some of his more hyper-clerical brethren by a black neck-handkerchief.[58]

Not only is there a hierarchy among lay society, but, by contrast, yet no less significant, it exists also among the members of the clergy.

Reading about how dress codes are played out and negotiated between different classes in novels of the late eighteenth and nineteenth centuries – precisely the period when the impact of the French Revolution and of the changes described in Chapter 3 as a result of technological innovation were making themselves felt – reveals that relationships between fashion and class changed more subtly than might otherwise be assumed from an exclusively 'economic' interpretation. It does not necessarily follow that just because cotton clothing became cheaper and more easily available, everyone wanted, or was able, to dress in it. The fact that George Eliot looks back from the late 1850s to twenty or so years previously, often making comparisons between contemporary society and the time of her early adulthood, is telling; like so many 'historical' novels, her focus is really the present and not the past, or at least the past in relation to the present. Comments made by George Eliot's characters such as linen being better than 'shop-rag', or indeed Elizabeth Gaskell's comment in the letter to her daughter about cotton – but *not* silk – being acceptable as a gift for a servant, show how fluid change was at this time and that codes relating to fabric and clothing were in flux. No wonder then that people wanted to assert and maintain their outward material association and identity with their own class.

Finally, Wilkie Collins (1824–1889) uses his image of the mysterious woman in white, Ann Catherick, encountered at the start of the novel of that name, to draw his readers into a complex plot built on suspense and intrigue. In *The Woman in White* (1859) both Ann Catherick and the heroine Laura Fairlie wear white muslin in order for Collins to exploit for the purpose of his plot their mistaken identities over the course of the novel. But they also wear white to contrast with the burlesque figure of Count Fosco and Mrs Catherick, whose base motives and actions are reflected in their adoption of *black* clothing. But aside from these rather simplistic associations of particular colours with good and bad – symbolic associations nevertheless that readers would have understood – Collins shows the complexity of class revealed in clothing. Early in the novel, for example, Laura is described as wearing simple white muslin deliberately to *disguise* her wealth, such is the delicacy of her sensibilities, especially in relation to her close companion Marian Halcombe whom she does not wish to make feel in any way inferior. There are wildcards in literature, as there are in life: the individual who does not conform to what is expected of them in relation to their class and status.

The title of Wilkie Collins's less well-known novel *No Name* describes its theme; it is an indictment of the laws of inheritance and of the consequences of having 'no name'. Here the wildcard is Captain Wragge, who tries to help the heroine Magdalen recover her name and social standing, less out of altruism, but more in an attempt to benefit himself and his wife. Captain Wragge's clothes have clearly seen better days, his name a deliberate play-on-words describing the state of his clothes and those of his wife:

> His dingy white collar and cravat had died the death of old linen, and had gone to their long home at the paper-maker's, to live again one day in quires at a stationer's shop. A grey shooting-jacket, in the last stage of woollen atrophy, replaced the black frock-coat of former times, and, like a faithful servant, kept the dark secret of its master's linen from the eyes of a prying world. From top to toe, every square inch of the captain's clothing was altered for the worse; but the man himself remained unchanged – superior to all forms of moral mildew, impervious to the action of social rust.[59]

It comes as no surprise that when Captain Wragge raises his hands he displays 'a pair of darned black gloves'.[60] So it is ironic when he repeatedly tells Mrs Wragge that she is 'down at heel':

> 'Do I hear a clapping on the floor!' exclaimed Captain Wragge, with an expression of horror. 'Yes; I do. Down at heel again! The left shoe this time. Pull it up, Mrs Wragge! Pull it up!'[61]

And shortly after this, he exclaims that *both* of her shoes are 'down at heel'.[62] Clearly this anxiety is contagious and Mrs Wragge, soon after her husband's accusation, describes *herself* as 'all down at heel'.[63] The earliest known use of the idiom 'down at heel' is thought to be in William Darrell and George Hickes's *A Gentleman Instructed in the Conduct of a Virtuous and Happy Life* (1732). The phrase is derived from the literal sense that if one's shoe heels were worn down, this was the most visible indication that someone was poor and could not afford new clothes; but it came to imply that someone was generally badly off and perhaps also that one's economic standing had been reduced. We learn that Captain Wragge had invested in the railways but lost out, reflecting a dynamic society with opportunities for making wealth, but also with substantial risks of losing it.

The Wragges refer repeatedly to the state of their clothing – a constant niggle for them and a reminder of their impoverished status. Mrs Wragge – like other characters we have encountered such as Jane Austen's Miss Steele and Elizabeth Gaskell's Manchester factory girls – has what verges on an obsessive interest in other people's clothing. She saves money by trying to make herself an 'Oriental Cashmere Robe'; 'I've got my patterns, and my dressmaking directions written out as plain as print', she says.[64] Magdalen, who, in spite of losing her name and inheritance, has been brought up not to have to make her own clothes, 'she who had hated the sight of her needle and thread, in old times – who had never yet worn an article of dress of her own making' – assists Mrs Wragge in this endeavour.[65] In her darkest moments, Magdalen thinks that clothing cannot change one's status if in one's mind one is 'worthless': in the process of trying to decide which of her two muslin dresses to put on she says, 'What does it matter! ... I am equally worthless in my own estimation, whichever I put on.'[66] 'Shall I tell you what a lady is?' she asks. 'A lady is a woman who wears a silk gown, and has a sense of her own importance.'[67] Later on in the novel she dresses as her servant, showing that clothing indicates class and status at least on a superficial level, and can be a useful disguise.[68]

This chapter has focused on selected writing that reflects a society in transition as a result of technological, economic and social change that was linked in large part to developments in the cotton industry from the end of the eighteenth century that altered the way many people lived and worked, dressed and consumed fashion. While these changes were undoubtedly momentous in the longer term, they did not bring about immediately as great a degree of class levelling as has perhaps been assumed. Perceptions of class and its relationship with particular fabrics and clothing articulated by a variety of novelists of the period reveal that, if anything, class distinctions became, over the nineteenth century, more pronounced as contrasts between urban and rural, north and south, were highlighted. For example, factory employment brought different classes into contact – and often conflict – in a more direct way and in the novels of Elizabeth Gaskell, the adoption of particular fabrics and attitudes towards dress was often perceived as gauges of social class. While cotton had the potential to be a powerful class leveller, we have seen how groups held on to the associations of more 'traditional' fabrics, such as linen and silk, as a way of distinguishing themselves from the classes thought to be beneath them and/or in order to articulate respectability and in the wake of new retail practices which were replacing timeworn methods of acquiring clothing. Meanwhile, the 'respectable' working classes, the middle classes and the landowning gentry were all anxious to maintain distinction between themselves and the class(es) beneath them. However, and as Anthony Trollope shows in *The Warden*, class was not the only determinant of the adoption of 'new' or more 'traditional' fabrics, but age was: 'The party went off as such parties do: there were fat old ladies, in fine silk dresses, and slim young ladies, in gauzy muslin frocks.'[69]

The late-eighteenth- and early-nineteenth-century novels constitute a fertile ground for accessing perceptions about class in its relation to fabric and clothing. However, by the beginning of the twentieth century, as Peter Keating points out, there was a growing preference for a fictional reality achieved by going beyond realism which 'reversed the central trend of British fiction as it had developed from the early eighteenth century' while 'the increasing openness of society at the close of the nineteenth century and the increasingly open narrative forms of early modern fiction go hand in hand.'[70] The next chapter will turn from literature and consider new manufacturing and retailing practices from the last decades of the nineteenth century and their role in democratising fashion.

5

Fashion, class and democratisation

To buy the thing, ready-made, is the taste of the day.

William Cobbett, *Rural Rides*[1]

When William Cobbett referred to the 'taste of the day' for ready-made goods in *Rural Rides* (1830), the mass production of clothing still had a long way to go. One hundred years later, Aldous Huxley, articulating the desire for the new and *distaste* for old and mended clothing, wrote in *Brave New World* (1932): 'I do love having new clothes, I do love ... But old clothes are beastly ... We always throw away old clothes. Ending is better than mending, ending is better than, mending, ending is better.'[2] By the mid-twentieth century the democratisation of clothing was almost complete. This chapter describes that transition in relation to class.

Previously, I referred to the political upheavals in America and France in the late eighteenth century along with the implications of new technologies that made possible the mass production of cotton fabric and clothing and how, together, they seemed to set in train the development of a more 'classless' society, at least as far as material and visual appearances were concerned. Certainly the potential for the democratisation of dress in the longer term was there, but changes were more gradual than is often assumed and created, in the shorter term, a more visibly *un*equal society, in which different classes often reasserted the sartorial superiority they had over the class or classes below them in the social hierarchy. Although social class distinctions may have grown subtler over the course of the Victorian period (1837–1901), they did not disappear. This is borne out by people's perceptions of the interaction between fabric, fashion and class in the nineteenth-century novel, as it is by photography of the period, Sarah Levitt arguing that 'the rigid class system was nowhere more apparent than in clothing, through which power, wealth and status were expressed.[3] Diana Crane cites data from empirical sociologist Pierre Guillaume Frédéric Le Play (1806–1882) whose research undertaken in England in the 1850s on the wardrobes of working-class men reveals disparities between the clothes of even the more fashionable of them and those of the upper middle class. Notwithstanding the increased availability of ready-made cotton clothing from the end of the eighteenth century, the numbers of items in these wardrobes and the frequency with which new items were added to them are strikingly different. Crane concludes that 'fashionable clothing as adopted by the working classes was a veneer rather than a way of life'.[4] So while the 'democratisation thesis' seems correct in a very literal sense, it hides the subtleties and nuances of fashion in its relationships with class.

By the final decades of the nineteenth century, however, new urban structures and cultures routinely influenced the regionalism of the English countryside, often reflected in contemporary comments about the ways in which the trend towards fashionable clothing acquired and worn by the (rural) working classes in the late nineteenth century was a kind of downgrading of traditional culture, associated with 'artificial' values emanating from the town. In his essay 'The Dorsetshire Labourer' (1883), Thomas Hardy (1840–1928) compares a Dorchester hiring fair of the time with one twenty or thirty years previously. Hardy observes how the traditional smock-frock, along with clothing that indicated occupation – and thereby class too – has disappeared and that now the 'crowd is as dark as a London crowd'.[5] Democratisation was as much the result of changing tastes and desires of working- and middle-class people for novelty, fashion and more material *things*, as it was the 'inevitable' consequence of new production processes.

Not only have debates about the erosion of class as defined by dress been 'silent on the extent of variations in appearance at different social class levels',[6] but they have also generally focused more on men than on women in this period. As far as middle-class men were concerned, a distinctly uniform look based on the dark suit, coat and hat became a 'badge' for professionals, captains of industry and even for the more artistic sections of Victorian society. The social reformer Beatrice Webb betrays her own consciousness of the reality of class when she describes in her diary her future husband, Sidney Webb:

A remarkable little man with a huge head on a very tiny body, a breadth of forehead quite sufficient to account for the encyclopaedic character of his knowledge, a Jewish nose, prominent eyes and mouth, black hair, somewhat unkempt, spectacles and a most *bourgeois* (my italics) black coat shiny with wear.[7]

Jennifer Craik observes that the development of the class system as an outcome of economic growth and restructuring coincided with changing perceptions of gender. With it came increasing identification of a particular class – the bourgeoisie – with the attributes of the 'feminine', newly defined in terms of the domestic and private sphere: 'Women were the visible correlate of the economic and social standing of their menfolk.'[8] This may be one reason why the move towards uniformity has been more frequently associated with men in the Victorian period, and not unrelated to this is the fact that the industry in men's ready-made clothing developed more quickly than that for women. The development of the ready-to-wear clothing system and new retailing practices of the second half of the nineteenth century are therefore the focus of this and the following chapters; together, they turned the potential for democratisation into a reality. In describing them, we move from the latter decades of the nineteenth century well into the twentieth. Thus, with the aftermath of the First World War came a degree of social levelling that was perhaps unprecedented. H. Llewellyn Smith remarked of the London West End in 1930:

The visible signs of class distinction are disappearing. Chokers, Derby coats and ostrich feathers are rarely to be seen. The dress of the younger generation of working men and women, so far from having any distinctive note of its own, tends merely to copy, and sometimes to exaggerate, any particular fashion current in the West End. In the same way paint and powder, once regarded in this class as the marks of the prostitute, are freely used by respectable working girls.[9]

Democratisation and the high street

The work of Christopher Breward, Edwina Ehrman and Caroline Evans together considers the democratisation of fashionable dress in relation to the high street; they argue that what happens there can influence what happens on the catwalk. Meanwhile Frank Mort's work on the retailing of the mass-produced suit and the Burton's menswear multiple has helped to establish the high street as a site of fashion culture.[10] Ben Fine and Ellen Leopold usefully define the fashion system as a 'dual' system of provision because of the 'interrelationship between highly fragmented forms of production and equally diverse and often volatile patterns of demand'. Fashion is therefore a 'hybrid' subject, since it is both a 'cultural phenomenon' and 'an aspect of manufacturing with the accent on production technology'.[11] By focusing both on the technology that changed the production processes of clothing and the way in which that clothing was then retailed by the new chains that grew to maturity in the period following the Second World War, high-street fashion altered irrevocably any simple correlation between upper- or middle-class status with fashionable, made-to-measure garments (made from expensive fabrics), and working-class status with badly fitting garments (made from cheaper, poor-quality fabrics). In this redefinition, an analysis based on the dynamics of demand and consumption must interact with those of production. This realignment has altered the perspectives we adopt when explaining historical change.

Histories published since the 1980s have challenged orthodoxies in economic history with its emphasis on supply- or production-focused explanations. For example, Neil McKendrick, John Brewer and Roy Porter's 1982 study *The Birth of a Consumer Society: The Commercialization of Eighteenth-Century England* and John Brewer and Roy Porter's 1993 study *Consumption and the World of Goods* offer critiques of historical approaches that have been far more interested in explaining 'how and why supply increased than in explaining how and why the products of that rising tide of industrial production were absorbed by the market'.[12] Neil McKendrick argues that, as early as the eighteenth century, fashion filtered down to all classes.[13] Some have criticised McKendrick for his privileging of the trickle-down theory, which, in this particular context, relies on the supposed emulation by domestic servants of upper-class styles in which the tastes of the latter are paramount while the specific consumption habits of the labouring classes are ignored.[14] It is also possible that the contribution to the erosion of class difference as a result of the passing down of clothes to servants from their employers has been exaggerated. Even as late as the 1860s, the diarist Arthur J. Munby comments on the social divide that always existed between himself and maid-of-all-work Hannah Cullick (even though in dress and demeanour she looks 'quite as refined' as a 'conventional lady') with whom he has a lasting friendship and love affair and whom he eventually marries:

> Monday 29th July 1861 … I went up at five o'clock to the Paddington Station. Hannah came there by 6.30: and after a word in private, we separated. She waited, walked about the platform, leaned on a rail, stood close by me: but always we were strangers: no look betrayed her; she neither expected nor wished me to notice her … She is content to pay for an actual nearness with an apparent contrast, which after all is natural on her side. And yet, in her straw bonnet and brown shawl and pink cotton frock (given her ten years ago by her mistress) she looked, not indeed a conventional lady, but something quite as refined.[15]

However, McKendrick's work highlights the important role of clothing in history. By implication he also questions any simplistic correlation between poverty and unfashionable clothing and its converse – wealth and access to fashionable clothing. Meanwhile Beverly Lemire's fascinating account of the expansion of the cotton industry details the history of the demand for cheaper cotton clothing and accessories made from a huge range of prints and colours from about 1760 onwards; the complex distribution and retailing networks that brought these goods to working-class populations in town and countryside and the ways in which fashion news in print was communicated. Together, this fuelled increased desire for novelty and consumption of the products of the Lancashire cotton industry. In other words, the technological progress that made all this possible went hand in hand with increased demand and one stimulated the other in a reciprocal relationship of supply and demand.

What do we mean by democratisation as applied to fashion? The term is generally used to describe an 'eventual standardization of clothing in which social class differences would be less visible or nonexistent',[16] or, as 'the process by which fashion and style, rather than being primarily the preserve of the rich, become increasingly accessible to a broader range of people than hitherto, in a diverse range of social and economic circumstances'.[17] Democratisation meant that the provision of clothing by chain-store multiples such as Marks & Spencer that expanded in the 1920s and 1930s enabled the emulation by working-class people of the styles of quality clothing consumed by the middle and upper classes. It is important because, whatever its future may be, *high-street fashion* has become so much a part of British, and indeed global, culture that it is hard to imagine a time when both it and its extension (online shopping) did not exist. The pioneering of new technical, design and marketing processes has altered radically the consumer's perception over time of what fashion means. Retailers began not only to interpret upper-end design, but also to create a new dynamic for fashionable change, which was determined less by class and economic means, but more by standardisation, albeit disguised by the illusion of choice. For better or worse, without Woolworth and Marks & Spencer, for example, there would probably be no Primark, no Zara and so on.

Complex though it is, the concept of democratisation is useful when discussed in relation to the clothing industry; it can reconcile issues around the traditional separation in academic discourse of the *production* of fabric and clothing and those factors that are linked to *consumption*. In the past, the divisions between histories of production and those of consumption have tended to result in a 'top downwards' perspective on fashion with little acknowledgement of 'ordinary' fashion, where trickle-down models of fashionable change are prioritised over those where changes 'bubble up' from working-class styles. The shortcoming of an exclusively economic interpretation of the technological changes in the cotton industry (discussed in Chapter 3) is that it emphasises the production of cotton fabric without considering associated demand and how it was consumed. Innovation – whether it is of a new fabric or of a new manufacturing process – is not sufficiently explained without consideration of patterns of consumption. For example, in Britain, on the one hand, one factor holding up the development and positive reception of ready-made clothing was that it was often associated with poor quality. In the United States, on the other hand, the emergence of mass production of clothing went hand in hand with effective retailing and marketing.

The development of the ready-to-wear clothing industry and the wholesale bespoke trade

Social identification through clothing was for centuries one of the underpinnings of European society … Commerce, however, made fashionable dress less a signal of the courtier's standing or the landowner's station, and more a commodity in the public domain, access to which was determined through objective criteria.

Beverly Lemire, *Fashion's Favourite*[18]

In Britain the context for the development and expansion of the ready-to-wear clothing industry was a growing population: England's population grew from 8.3 million in 1801 to 30.5 million a century later, while Scotland and Wales witnessed a similar expansion, the population growing to 4.5 million in Scotland and 2 million in Wales by 1901.[19] Before the 1870s, when ready-made clothing became more readily and cheaply available (especially for men), only a very small proportion of working-class people bought new clothes, so the second-hand clothes trade was vitally important for the provision of relatively cheap and respectable clothing.[20] The ascendancy of new clothes over good second-hand items only took place well after the turn of the twentieth century. Melanie Tebbutt's study of pawnbroking in the nineteenth century gives a useful account of the role of clothing in creating working-class credit through pawning and of the subsequent decline of pawnshops in the context of the expansion of the ready-to-wear clothing industry which made cheap clothing available and also undermined the easy disposal of second-hand clothing.[21] However, 'ready-made' at this time was often synonymous with 'poor quality', and in both fit and fabric considered generally inferior to second-hand.

It is important to distinguish between the development of ready-made clothing in general and factory-made clothing. Placing too much emphasis on the latter and its association with the second half of the nineteenth century has meant that the earlier history of the industry – which is in fact older than has often been assumed – has been underplayed.[22] Beverly Lemire, however, argues that the mass market was well established by 1800 and with this, 'the visual distinctions between the ranks narrowed as a result [of the dissemination of popular fashions], blurring further social differentiation'.[23] For example, her work evidences the sale of ready-made cotton gowns as early as the 1760s and 1770s.[24] Ellen Leopold also argues that mass markets preceded mass production (in a limited sense).[25] By the 1930s, the ready-made garment industry was therefore at least 150 years old. Even so, at the beginning of the twentieth century, its development was hampered by production 'issues' as well as by an image problem. On the one hand, the technical application of machinery to the clothing industry as a whole was uneven. The textile industry, in contrast to the apparel industry, showed all the classic features of mass production: it was heavily capitalised, highly concentrated and operated in large-scale production units.[26] The clothing industry, on the other hand, was labour-intensive, and continued to rely on the individually operated sewing machine well into the twentieth century.[27] Furthermore, the industrial manufacture of women's clothing was a long way behind that of men's clothing, even at the close of the First World War.

In the eighteenth century, ready-made clothes could be purchased from special 'show shops'. Sailors in particular demanded clothing of simple construction that could be worn immediately, often referred to as 'slops'.[28] By the beginning of the nineteenth century, 'slop shops' had become well established.[29] The Napoleonic Wars (1793–1815) stimulated growth in government contracts for cheap army and navy clothing. Middlemen employed workers (mainly women) to mass-produce garments in their own homes or in workshops for very little pay.[30] The Leeds ready-made clothing industry developed rapidly from the 1860s, where production was divided between the making of trousers (mostly in factories housing early sewing machines, which stitched only straight lines) and of jackets (performed mostly in Jewish workshops by skilled Jewish tailors).[31] Many of the early outlets for ready-made clothing enjoyed a far from respectable reputation. Shoddy cloth (made from recycled wool, cotton and mixtures) became the staple of the developing ready-to-wear clothing industry; the association of shoddy cloth with poor quality was partly responsible for giving the embryonic ready-to-wear clothing industry a bad reputation. The nineteenth-century social commentator Henry Mayhew was less than complimentary of the show and slop shops, comparing them unfavourably with tailoring outlets for bespoke (individually ordered) clothing. Even in the early twentieth century a similar attitude is well illustrated by Arnold Bennett in his novel *The Old Wives' Tale* (1908). By the end of the novel, the former drapery store in the Staffordshire pottery town of Bursley (based on Burslem) has been taken over by the Midland Clothiers Company and is selling ready-made coats. Not only does the shop's advertising techniques shock residents, but the cheapness of the coats presents formidable competition to those still in the business of bespoke tailoring. The following extract illustrates something of the provincial conservatism in dress and shopping habits and the antipathy towards ready-made clothing at the beginning of the twentieth century:

> The tailoring of the world was loudly and coarsely defied to equal the value of those overcoats … Twelve-and-sixpenny overcoats! It was monstrous, and equally monstrous was the gullibility of the people. How could an overcoat at twelve and sixpence be 'good'? She [Constance] remembered the overcoats made and sold in the shop in the time of her father and her husband, overcoats of which the inconvenience was that they would not wear out! The Midland, for Constance, was not a trading concern, but something between a cheap-jack and a circus.[32]

The ingrained prejudice against ready-made, 'off-the-peg' clothing is explained both by its association with poor quality as well as by the fact that women's body-hugging styles of the nineteenth century meant that a perfect fit – implying respectability and gentility – was more likely to be achieved by made-to-measure clothing. Underneath this clothing, corsets, which were adopted by women who were mostly aristocrats and the urban upper middle class, gave a smooth and sylphlike figure to the small number of women (probably less than 5 per cent) who wore them.[33] The services of either a dressmaker, or, in a minority of cases, a couturier, could be afforded only by the upper classes and aspiring middle classes; well-fitting clothing was therefore confirmation of class and status. Ready-made accessories such as stockings, shawls or mantles were, however, acceptable purchases from a department store. This prejudice helps to explain why the sectors of the women's ready-to-wear garment industry that developed most quickly were those where fit was relatively unimportant, that is, where the garment was, by its nature, loose fitting (a mantle), or where it could be sold partly made up (a skirt or bodice) and could be altered according to the wearer's specific measurements.

The earliest wholesale mantle manufactory in the City of London is thought to have been D. Nicholson of King William Street in 1837. Even before this, however, it was possible to buy part-made dresses, which the customer's own dressmakers could finish to fit.[34] Elizabeth Wilson and Lou Taylor point out that

part-made bodices were for sale as early as the 1830s.[35] We have also seen how
Beverly Lemire's analysis dates ready-made gowns for working-class women to
some seventy years before *that*. Women's underwear could be bought ready-
made from as early as the 1840s, although it was, for the most part, stitched by
hand well into the twentieth century. However, manufacturers did not really
start to explore the full potential of ready-to-wear clothing for women until the
1870s.[36] In her work on the history of mourning dress, Lou Taylor has shown
how the provision of clothing by well-known mourning warehouses such as
Jay's in Regent Street, London, 'encouraged the development of ready to-wear
clothes for middle- and upper-class clients' and that by 1910, completely ready-
made dresses were available.[37] Indeed, by the end of the nineteenth century,
some areas of the ready-made clothing industry were flourishing.

Two of the best-known family firms catering to the male ready-made
clothing trade were Elias Moses & Son Ltd of Aldgate and Minories (established
in 1834) and Hyam & Company. Originally second-hand clothes dealers with
links to the ready-made tailoring trade, they established themselves in the
City of London before opening West End branches. As well as fashionable off-
the-peg garments for men who wanted the kind of clothing worn by higher
social classes, they supplied uniforms, servants' liveries, workwear, outfits for
emigrants, mourning clothes and some women's clothing.[38] Pamela Sharpe
draws attention to Hyam's 1828 handbills advertising ready-made clothing
for working men, including, for example, fustian trousers, jackets, beaverteen
trousers and coats.[39]

One of the key factors in the development of the mass production of ready-
made clothing during the second half of the nineteenth century was the
introduction of a viable sewing machine that could be applied to large-scale
factory production. Although the earliest known patent for a sewing machine
was granted in 1790 to Thomas Saint, a London cabinet-maker, it is probable
that Saint never actually constructed a machine and that his theoretical
drawings, had they been translated into a machine, would not have been
viable.[40] A large number of the developments in sewing machines which were
to have a major impact on the clothing industry were pioneered in the United
States: between 1842 and 1895, a staggering 7,339 patents for sewing machines
and accessories were issued.[41] The first really practical sewing machine was
patented by Elias Howe (Figure 5.1) in Boston in 1846, a machine which

Figure 5.1 Elias Howe, by Albert Sands Southworth (1811–1894) and Josiah Johnson Hawes (1808–1901), *ca.* 1850. Daguerreotype (Bettmann/Getty Images).

produced only a lockstitch. Some years later, in 1851, Isaac Merrit Singer introduced a sewing machine from the United States into Britain, developing (in 1854) for the first time a machine with a continuous stitch and forward cloth-feed (Figure 5.2).

It is likely that the first entirely machine-made dresses were made in the home. However, in the 1850s and 1860s, factories were beginning to house the new sewing machines: John Barran's famous clothing factory in Leeds – where the clothing trade was one of the most advanced in the country – was probably the first factory to use the sewing machine in around 1856.[42] In the 1840s, Barran had two workshops producing both bespoke and some ready-made garments. In the 1850s, however, he opened his first factory in Alfred Street, Leeds, producing ready-to-wear garments. By 1867 he had moved to larger premises, with stock to the value of £10,000; by this date almost all the goods

Figure 5.2 A trade card advertising a manufacturing shop selling sewing machines, threads and cotton, *ca.* 1880 (photo by Bob Thomas/Popperfoto/Getty Images).

were ready-made.[43] In these factories, the sewing machines were linked to a central shaft that provided steam power. By the 1870s, gas, and later electricity, was used as the source of power. In other areas of the industry, innovations were also taking place. For example, the introduction of a buttonholing machine and, in 1875, a button-sewer quickened the pace at which tailoring tasks could be carried out. However, these innovations did not increase the number of garment pieces that could be worked on simultaneously and it was only with the introduction of the steam-powered cutting knife in the 1870s that machinists could be supplied with the requisite quantities of cut-out pieces, thus significantly speeding up the production process.[44]

Notwithstanding the importance of technical innovation (the sewing machine and the cutting knife or 'band knife' in particular) in facilitating the growth of the ready-to-wear clothing industry, subsequently the development of the industry relied on increasing labour intensification, especially the exploitation of female labour.[45] In 1891, for example, women comprised between 70 and 80 per cent of the Leeds clothing workforce. Machining formed the bulk of women's work, but other 'female' tasks included binding, trimming, buttonholing and finishing.[46] According to the census of 1881, after domestic service and textiles, the clothing trades occupied the largest single category of paid work for women, mostly in workshops or in their own homes on an outwork basis.[47] In fact, the trade in ready-made clothing – as distinct from the textile industry, which was heavily mechanised – had always relied more on the supply of cheap and plentiful labour than on technology and for many years continued to do so.

While an analysis that considers new manufacturing and retailing practices offers valuable insights into a study of the relationship between fashion and class, we have seen in previous chapters how contemporary (fictional) literature adds a new dimension to the discussion. Moving from fiction to 'fact', the diaries and papers of Arthur J. Munby (1828–1910) kept at Trinity College Cambridge (where Munby had been a student) provide some fascinating insights into class and the ways in which class differences were played out in individual lives. Insightful for us is that Munby comments, often in great detail, on the clothing of working-class groups, including London milkwomen, the fisherwomen of Langwm (near Milford Haven), acrobats, the notorious (because they wore trousers at a time when this was highly unusual) pit-brow women of Wigan and, not least, domestic servants. Photographs of some of these women are also found in the Trinity College collection of his papers (Figures 5.3 and 5.4).

In particular Munby describes his beloved Hannah Cullick, employed as a maid-of-all-work for much of her working life. He makes frequent comparisons between the clothing worn by middle-class women who were his 'social equals' – from whose number he was expected to marry – and the humble clothing of women who had to work for a living. We are left in no doubt of his own preference when he writes: 'commend me to the honest roughness of a stolid maid of all work, rather than to the hybrid fineladyism of Miss Swan and Edgar'[48] (a reference to the well-known London department store). In a diary entry the following year, Munby questions the 'rationale' for class difference among the young women he talks to when he dines with friends in Clapham:

And all these young ladies, white bosomed, fairylike with muslin and flowers, found a foil for their elegance in a pretty but coarsemade rustic and redhanded waiting maid. Gentle, and beautiful in face as they – and her name Laura too – why should she have a life so different? Why should she wear a cotton frock and a cap and hand me dishes – why should those imperious misses order her about so?[49]

Figure 5.3 Female collier from Rose Bridge Pits, Wigan, *ca.* 1869. Trinity College, Cambridge, Munby Collection, 112/7c (Courtesy of the Master and Fellows of Trinity College Cambridge).

Although Munby is not necessarily dismissive of the new palette of colours made possible by the development of chemical dyes, he is often scathing about the 'form' of fashion. At Brandon's ('the great shop in Oxford Street'), he chooses a 'bonnet' with his younger sister:

I chose a structure of the period; ugly in all but colour and material (which are left free to the worshipper's choice, who is thereby the more enslaved

Figure 5.4 Hannah Cullick, maid-of-all-work, cleaning boots. Trinity College, Cambridge, Munby Collection, 114/3a (Courtesy of the Master and Fellows of Trinity College Cambridge).

as to the *form*) and destined to look ridiculous ten years hence. Colour, 'Magenta'; price, 25/-; cheap, I am told! ... went and bought a trifle for my Hannah. 'A nice present for a servant, Sir,' said the man: so *he* knew too![50]

While we do not know what the present was, Munby's account is evidence of the hierarchy of gifts and purchases in relation to class. The following year he describes the dress of a London milkwoman (plain, straw bonnet, woollen shawl and clean cotton frock, but her bonnet 'wanted the thick white cap', her boots were 'effeminately thin' and her gown reached her ankles) and Munby suggests that 'fashion' might be 'infecting' this group of workers, but at the same time he also draws a 'delicious' contrast between the milkwoman and a 'mincing' lady with 'tiny hands in lavender kid'.[51] In July 1862, Hannah and Munby were thinking of holidaying together; Hannah suggests that she dresses up in men's clothes since on the one hand she cannot possibly be seen with Munby in her servant's clothes yet, on the other hand, she cannot go dressed as a lady. This is a strong indication of their class difference as revealed by clothing.[52] He frequently makes reference to the stares of onlookers if he is walking together with Hannah.[53] Or of how, when they meet, they have to avoid being in the presence of Munby's friends or acquaintances. On other occasions he describes the sharp contrast between the gangs of Paddington dustwomen near Apsley House in fustian jackets and the 'troop of exquisites' in faultless gloves and sumptuous attire and aristocratic moustaches and 'belles' who 'lay supine' under a 'cloud of pink and white fluff in the barouches that waited near, the latter two groups not taking heed of the dustwomen'.[54]

For all Munby's desire for there to be no class divide between himself and 'his' Hannah, on a number of occasions, his views reflect his own ingrained class consciousness. In June 1869 he observes the Queen's 'Grand Review' of troops in Windsor Park, noticing that most of the onlookers are Londoners ('no smockfrocks') but many maidservants from Windsor and he observes how the latter are distinguishable, if not by their clothes, then by their hands, which

> show work; and if gloved, you still see they are larger than a lady's … her dress is less costly than a lady's, less tasteful than a milliner's; yet is an imitation of fashionable attire … But how incongruous to see such a girl, wearing quasiladylike dress that well became her had she known how to wear it, to see her all gauche and careless … More culture, such a girl wants, or more rusticity.[55]

Even after he and Hannah were married on 14 January 1873 (Hannah wearing a simple servant's 'frock'[56]), Munby did not acknowledge her in public as his wife and Hannah mostly found it hard to call him her husband even in private. For trips together he buys her clothes so that she will appear to be 'a lady' but she is never as comfortable as she is in her servant's frock with her arms bare, apron and cotton cap. They later lived apart, though Munby visited Hannah frequently after she moved to her last home, a cottage in Shifnal, Shropshire. She died in 1909 and was buried in Shifnal churchyard, where in due course an inscription on a stone kerb commemorated 'Hannah for 36 years the beloved wife and servant of Arthur Joseph Munby'. It is a remarkable and moving story of how great and enduring love could not bridge the still-insurmountable class divide in the latter half of the nineteenth century.

From around 1900, large-scale production of ready-made suits was augmented by the manufacture of wholesale bespoke suits – made-to-measure suits that could be sold at the same price as their ready-made equivalent. From the mid-1880s, both Joseph Hepworth & Sons and William Blackburn (established 1867) began to sell ready-made and made-to-measure through their own retail outlets. Katrina Honeyman observed that David Little was perhaps the first company to recognise the potential of developing a 'special measure' or 'special order' department, whereby customers' measurements and their selection of cloth were conveyed to one of the factories or workshops of the large wholesale companies for making up.[57] Like Michael Marks (co-founder of Marks & Spencer), Meshe David Osinsky (born 1885) was an immigrant and pedlar (of flannel suits). Having first opened a hosiery and drapery shop in Chesterfield in 1904, Montague Burton – as he now called himself – entered the bespoke trade in 1906. Advertising in the *Derbyshire Times* in 1906 (14 April), men's suits were noted for their 'hard wear and perfect fit' (prices from 11s. 9d.) while boys' suits were available 'in endless variety' and retailed from 1s. 9d.[58]

The distinguishing feature of the multiple tailors, as they became known, was the integration of the manufacturing and retailing of men's tailored outerwear. They opened networks of shops supplied by their own factory production and 'played a key role in extending the social and geographical distribution of men's tailored outerwear … For the first time, ordinary working people could afford to buy new tailored woollen clothing comparable with that worn by the middle and upper class'.[59] Like Marks & Spencer, it was in the interwar period that the multiples really expanded, providing 'about a third of all tailored clothing for British men'.[60] They came to dominate the high street. By 1939 Montague Burton Ltd owned nearly 600 shops,[61] taking over from Hepworth, who prior to the First World War had been the largest manufacturer and distributor of men's clothes.[62] During this period, the relatively small number of firms producing womenswear, such as Heaton & Co. (established 1900), were also successful.[63] Frank Mort argues, however, that the clothing multiples such as Burton's, and the wholesale bespoke trade in general, continued to imitate the aristocratic protocols of the genuine bespoke tailors of Savile Row in their approach to customers: 'Burton's suits were factory-made, employing strictly standardized procedures, but "sir" was measured by Burton's salesmen with all the ritual of a traditional tailoring establishment.'[64] The firm's emphasis, argues Mort, was therefore as much on continuity and tradition as on innovation.[65] In this respect Burton and other retailers of wholesale bespoke suits therefore aligned themselves with traditional retailing practices. While the wholesale bespoke trade in men's clothing and its retailing via outlets such as Burton's and Hepworth provide a useful point of comparison with the retail practices of Marks & Spencer, Fine and Leopold argue that the early arrival of mass production and marketing of men's clothing derives less from the tradition of bespoke tailoring than from the early ready-to-wear markets (in the late eighteenth century) for cheap work clothes (discussed earlier) for those without access to tailoring services, for example, sailors, slaves, indentured servants, domestic servants and those building the nation's infrastructure – the navvies (builders of canals and subsequently railways).[66] Taking a case-study approach, the next chapter will discuss the development of Marks & Spencer, in particular its contribution to the democratisation of women's clothing.

6

Retailing revolution: Marks & Spencer and the democratisation of fashion

In Britain the 1920s were seminal to the democratisation of clothing because it was at this time that Marks & Spencer (founded 1884), F. W. Woolworth (founded 1909), Littlewoods (founded 1923) and British Home Stores (founded 1928) were either established, or, in the case of Marks & Spencer, began to concentrate on the retailing of *clothing*. By 1939 these chains together had around twelve hundred stores in Britain, commanding nearly 20 per cent of the total sales achieved by multiple retail organisations.[1] However, the primary focus of dress historians and fashion commentators and journalists in the twentieth century was frequently on the top end of the fashion business and on the significance of high-profile fashion designers, in spite of the fact that, as Susannah Frankel estimated for the late 1990s, there were fewer than 2,000 customers worldwide who bought the most expensive made-to-measure clothing.[2]

The decision by Marks & Spencer to sell clothing on a large scale from the mid-1920s and the sheer range of products available in stores only a decade later – in particular working-class women's clothing – reveal how retailers were able to respond to, and stimulate, technological developments within the ready-to-wear clothing industry. This shift to clothing reflects changes in class structures and social roles as well as in the lifestyles of women for whom fashion might not have been considered attainable previously. From the 1930s onwards, further technological and design developments affecting the quality and look of mass-produced clothing, coupled with changes in the retail environment and the 'shopping experience', along with new ways clothing retailers communicated with their customers, created the phenomenon of high-street clothing as we understand the term today.[3] The high-street multiples had not only responded to this new demand, but they had helped to create it.

Early development of Marks & Spencer

The success of Marks & Spencer in the interwar period probably exceeded the most optimistic expectations of the company's founder, Michael Marks (1863–1907) – who had emigrated from the village of Bialystok (then Russian Poland) probably not later than 1882, fleeing persecution of the Jews in one of a series of pogroms – and those of his son, Simon Marks (1888–1964). By 1884 Michael was in Leeds, a rapidly growing city with a population of 310,000, an important communications centre for the West Riding of Yorkshire and a hub of the mining, manufacturing and clothing industries. When he married Hannah Cohen in 1886, Michael Marks is described as a 'licensed hawker' on his marriage certificate, even though he had by this time given up peddling. The role of the itinerant salesman in supplying goods to people of humble means, living in remote villages and who visited the nearest town infrequently, at most on market day or for the annual fair, had been vitally important in the distribution of goods for centuries, even though the hawker's stock was modest compared with that of the 'Manchester Men' or 'Scotch Drapers'. According to a witness before a Royal Commission (1833), travelling salesmen 'call upon the families once in three weeks and I should think that half of the population get their clothing in that way'.[4] Some clothing items would have been ready-made such as stockings, shifts and petticoats for women and shirts for men. However, Michael's own modest pack probably consisted of goods such as buttons, mending wools, pins, needles, tapes, tablecloths, woollen socks and stockings – goods that reflected the domestic needs of people on low incomes whose clothes were largely made at home, or, if and when they could afford it, by the village dressmaker. In spite of the important role that travelling salesmen of all kinds continued to play in the second half of the nineteenth century, their number was declining.

It was probably for this reason that Michael Marks gave up peddling and instead opened a stall in the open market on Kirkgate in Leeds two days a week (Tuesdays and Saturdays), travelling on the other days to Castleford and Wakefield in order to expand his business. Before long, he was running a stall on the *covered* market, which was open for trading throughout the week and where he introduced his well-known slogan, 'Don't Ask the Price, It's a Penny', so that customers could select whatever they wanted without having to ask the price or haggle. The principle of self-selection of goods without having to mention cost made shopping 'respectable' for working-class customers. It was at this time that Michael went into partnership with Tom Spencer: Marks & Spencer was formed on 28 September 1894 and became a limited company in 1903.

Michael Marks's customers – both as a licensed hawker and then when he ran his market stalls – were working-class people on (low) incomes, averaging 15s. a week.[5] This sector of the market was becoming increasingly significant in terms of its purchasing power. The articles sold by Michael Marks fell mostly within the categories of haberdashery (e.g. skeins of wool, reels of black and white cotton, bundles of elastic, corset laces, safety pins, cards of buttons, darning needles, knitting needles and mushroom darners) and fancy goods (e.g. brooches, combs, handkerchiefs and bracelets). In fact, the items sold could include anything considered useful which fitted into the penny (1d.) price point. They reflect the necessity of home dressmaking aids at a time when the majority of poor people made and mended their own clothes or relied on second-hand clothing.

In 1897, the company's headquarters were moved from Wigan to Manchester and from then until the First World War, Marks & Spencer witnessed rapid expansion. By 1907 there were more than 60 branches distributed throughout northern England, the Midlands, Wales and London; then during the period from 1907 until 1914, the number of branches more than doubled to a total of 140. In addition, shops were beginning to outnumber 'Penny Bazaars' in market halls or arcades. The number of stores opened in London also increased. In 1916 Michael's son Simon became chairman and his childhood friend Israel Sieff became vice-chairman and joint managing director in 1926, the year in which Marks & Spencer became a public company.

Changes in the consumer market: Marks & Spencer's expansion into clothing, 1926–36

From the mid-1920s, the emphasis by the company on clothing for working-class people became increasingly important. Along with social and cultural changes in the aftermath of the First World War came the demand from women for less formal, more comfortable clothes, while the popular styles of the 1920s, with their looser fit, lent themselves more readily to mass production. Early sales records (known as 'checking lists') show that the company was selling items such as domestic servants' uniforms as well as men's work dungarees. Though not at this time in the same league as, say, Burton's and Hepworth, Marks & Spencer was attempting to make its clothing both affordable and respectable, in terms of price, quality and style.

By 1936 the textile side of the business accounted for two-thirds of the company's total sales, and by 1950 Marks & Spencer was classified by the Board of Trade as a 'clothing multiple'.[6] The company's transition from a provider of haberdashery, household necessities and fancy goods to a retailer of clothing had to counter the ingrained prejudices held by many towards ready-made garments and the relative backward state of the industry in Britain. By contrast, in the United States the ready-made clothing industry was much more advanced. In 1924 Simon Marks made a fact-finding trip to the United States which helped to confirm his vision for the future of Marks & Spencer. In his notes Simon referred to Sewell Avery, chairman of the American company Montgomery Ward.[7] Founded in 1872, Montgomery Ward initially sold exclusively by mail-order, tapping the huge potential clothing market (for men and boys in particular) of small-town residents and farmers. In the 1920s, it expanded rapidly and began to operate retail stores, becoming a substantial supplier of women's ready-made clothing. It comes as no surprise therefore that following Simon's return from the United States, Marks & Spencer's direction changed, from selling a wide range of goods that, up until 1915, fitted into the original penny price point, to concentrating on the retailing of *clothing*,

In 1928 Simon Marks introduced, among other things, a new pricing policy in the form of a five-shilling limit for the price of goods, the idea probably originating from the American utilisation of the one-dollar maximum. (Only with inflation and the outbreak of the Second World War was the five-shilling maximum abandoned.) For the time being, however, the new price limit meant that the company had to create a range of goods that would fit within it. The profit margin, even at the level of five shillings, was small enough to require that the volume and pace of sales remained high. As Israel Sieff recalls:

One of its effects [the five-shilling limit] was to make textiles, and particularly women's clothing, our most important and popular line. It drove out a vast range of goods – the 'jumble' as Simon referred to it – which did not fit the modern pattern, and brought the textiles in.[8]

Significantly haberdashery, which had been such an important staple of the company's trade from its very early days, disappeared in 1936. Other innovations at this time included the introduction of larger stores facilitating a more effective display of merchandise (especially of clothing) and the establishment of a system of sales and stock recording, later known as the 'Checking List System', which facilitated fortnightly reports on what was selling and what was not – an indispensable gauge of consumer demand and preference. As a result, clothing, according to Israel Sieff's son, Marcus, became the leading section of the business:

Our growth reflected the increase in the demand for clothes, especially women's; fewer women wanted to make their own clothes at home; they wanted variety and colour, and lighter clothing for leisure. To a lesser degree this applied for men too.[9]

Between 1925 and 1940, the growth of the sale of textiles was the 'greatest single feature in this great fifteen-year period of growth ... By 1940, textiles had become the biggest single section of the company's business, at least three times as large as any other'.[10]

The Marks & Spencer Company Archive at the University of Leeds retains a number of past checking lists. A rare one for February 1938 is for the store in Douglas, Isle of Man: it evidences the sheer variety and range of clothing sold at this time and the extent to which the company now prioritised clothing as follows: boys' wear (*sic*); men's wear (*sic*); wool and cotton underwear; ladies' art. [artificial] silk underwear; knitted outerwear; overalls and mackintoshes; skirts; dresses; blouses; ladies' hosiery; children's socks and boys' hose; men's hose; children's wear (*sic*); corsetry; gloves and millinery; leather footwear, rubber footwear and slippers. For each department, there is a list of individual descriptions of the garments being sold. The variety is astonishing. For example, the leather footwear department, a relatively new department which had undergone rapid expansion in the early 1930s, includes the following: babies', children's and ladies' shoes; boys' boots; youths' shoes; men's boots and shoes;

wellingtons; plimsolls; slippers. By all accounts Simon Marks was a visionary and astute businessman, ruthless when it came to eradicating lines that were unpopular. He recognised an untapped market for the provision of quality, ready-made clothes. While men of the lower-middle and working classes were already being catered for in terms of affordable clothing (both ready-made and wholesale bespoke suits) by shops such as Burton's and Hepworth (see Chapter 5), there was no real equivalent source of clothing for women.

Marks & Spencer's main competitor in the period immediately after the First World War was the well-known American giant, F. W. Woolworth. Frank Winfield Woolworth's 'great five-cent store' was opened in 1879; by 1905 the company was incorporated as F. W. Woolworth & Co., with 120 stores in the United States. The first 3d. (threepenny) and 6d. (sixpenny) stores were opened in England in 1909 (Liverpool), the company undergoing swift expansion so that by the end of 1912 there were an incredible 596 stores. As Marks & Spencer was a close competitor, Simon Marks and Israel Sieff must have been aware of the prices charged by Woolworth (the idea of the upper price limit was clearly an American practice, though not one that was exclusive to Woolworth). They would also have kept a close eye on the products sold by Woolworth and there must have been some urgency on the part of Marks & Spencer to counter the competition. In fact, in the early 1920s Marks & Spencer engaged some former Woolworth managers.[11]

The nature of women's clothing in the late nineteenth and early twentieth centuries compared to the relative uniformity of the male suit helps to explain the slow pace at which mass production was adopted for the manufacture of female clothing. The interwar years witnessed massive expansion of the total number of Burton's shops, fuelled partly by the demand for made-to-measure suits during the demobilisation of 1918–19, the mass produced male suit becoming an emblem of mass society, projecting an image of cultural democracy and collective masculine uniformity.[12] By 1925 Montague Burton's 'new' clothing factory, situated in Hudson Road, Leeds, was reputed to be the largest clothing factory in Europe, servicing by far the largest chain of textile stores in the world.[13] Women's fashions meanwhile were more diverse although the more loosely fitting styles of the 1920s were relatively easy to cut, construct and, significantly, size, while fashionable, lightweight fabrics such as silk jersey could be simulated in rayon for a fraction of the price.[14] In this context, the achievements of both the menswear multiples along with retailers such as Marks & Spencer that pioneered the mass provision of ready-made women's clothing are landmarks in the history of fashion and its relationship with class (Figure 6.1).

By the end of the nineteenth century, those drawing factory wages, in spite of often bad living conditions, were beginning to experience an improved standard of living with more disposable income as a result. Hamish Fraser has shown that, on the whole, the higher the income, the greater the proportion spent on clothing.[15] However, although working-class incomes rose in the last two decades of the nineteenth century, they did not rise as quickly in the early twentieth century.[16] Following the massive economic and social dislocation of the First World War, there was still desperate poverty and high unemployment in the 1920s and 1930s. However, new trends towards mass consumerism and increasing spending power of those in work (due to a fall in the cost of living) helps to explain the growing demand by working-class women for fashionable, quality, reasonably priced clothing. Meanwhile, changing social structures and work patterns meant that middle-class women in particular had less time for fittings, so that high-quality, ready-to-wear clothing became desirable across all classes. By 1939, according to Elizabeth Wilson and Lou Taylor, the cost of living was 11 per cent lower than in 1924, while average wage rates were 3.5 per cent higher.[17] This helps to explain how Marks & Spencer was able to maintain a five-shilling maximum on the price of clothing up until 1939.

Not only was this a formative period for chain-store expansion, making ready-made clothing available to working-class people, but it was also the heyday of London department stores in terms of their physical and corporate expansion. Catering largely for the middle market, Debenhams bought Marshall & Snelgrove in 1919, for example, and Selfridges' western extension opened in 1924, thus providing 14,163 square metres (3.5 acres) of floor space in the basement alone.[18] The visible signs of class distinction seemed to be disappearing in the 1920s and 1930s with a 'flattening out' of differences between the dress codes of the various classes which was especially visible in London. Even so, the impact on patterns of retailing made by the department stores in London and elsewhere was to make fashionable clothing more accessible to a *middle-class* clientele. These stores were still out of reach for most working-class people, so a source of cheaper ready-made clothing

Figure 6.1 Photograph of front exterior of Marks & Spencer store (48–50 Oldham Street, Manchester), 1920s/1930s. Catalogue no. P1/1/198/5 (courtesy of the M&S Company Archive, University of Leeds).

became especially important for women on low incomes for whom work required a smart appearance, but for whom long hours combined with family commitments gave them little time for anything else. For these women, the purchase of new (rather than second-hand) ready-made, reasonably priced, quality clothing became an aspiration and not just a necessity and this was the market companies such as Marks & Spencer tapped into.

Daisy Ward (born *ca.* 1911) recalls working in a Leicester hosiery factory in the late 1920s and 1930s, and describes a ten-hour working day with no lunch breaks or tea breaks: 'I used to go to Marks & Spencer's (*sic*) and get a nice skirt in the old days, it was nothing over five shillings in Marks & Spencer's. For ten shillings I was very well dressed.'[19] The in-house *Marks & Spencer Magazine* in 1932 carries an article, 'How to Get Two Pounds' Worth for a Pound: Mrs Goodwife Goes Out Shopping'! The piece is of its time: Mrs Goodwife is given £1 by her husband, and manages to buy essential items for her wardrobe. Her husband is so impressed that he gives her another £2 to buy clothes for the children and, finally, he goes to buy an outfit for himself.[20] The aim of the article, of course, was to promote the ways in which Marks & Spencer clothing offered exceptional value for money and how it therefore contributed to higher living standards. In 1936 Simon Marks told M&S shareholders:

> Goods and services once regarded as luxuries have become conventional comforts and are now almost decreed necessities. A fundamental change in people's habits has been brought about. Millions are enjoying a substantially higher standard of living. To this substantial rise in the standard of living our company claims to have made a definite contribution.[21]

It is interesting to note that companies which later became associated with the retailing of cheap, mass fashion, such as C&A, sold clothing at substantially higher prices than Marks & Spencer at this time.[22] In 1922 the Oxford Street store of C&A Modes celebrated its opening by advertising its merchandise as constituting 'the height of fashion at the lowest cost'.[23] Advertisements for C&A appear in the 1920s alongside those for other department stores: Selfridges (W1), Whiteley's (W2), Derry & Toms (W8) and Bon Marché, Brixton (SW9), for example.[24] C&A saw its customers in the same middle-class social 'set' as these, its more established, competitors. Marks & Spencer, however, began as a provider of working-class clothing and only later in the century did it become a repository of middle-class respectability, casting aside an earlier reputation that had placed it alongside Woolworth. That Marks & Spencer was catering for a working-class market at this time is confirmed by research into another source: the Hodson Shop Dress Collection, a rare collection of nearly 3,000 items of 1920s clothing surviving from the stock of a small shop in the town of Willenhall, West Midlands. In the late 1920s the clothing sold from this shop was priced from 4s. 11d. (the price for the cheapest 'tub' or washing-frocks), although the majority of the clothes were more expensive and out of the reach of factory girls.[25] Until 1939, the *upper* price limit at Marks & Spencer, therefore, was the same as the *lowest* at the Hodson shop.

As a retailer of goods for working-class people, Marks & Spencer can be seen in the same tradition as chains such as Lipton's – for grocery provision – and the Co-operative retail outlets. Co-operative retailing had flourished in the second half of the nineteenth century, especially in northern industrial towns. Analysis of Marks & Spencer's checking lists in the late 1930s reveals an astonishing variety of clothes sold by the company in this period. Examples of 'staple ranges' constituted, for example, underwear (locknit and interlock as opposed to the more 'glamorous' artificial silk and, even more desirable, real silk), hosiery, overalls and traditional bib and braces. In these lines of 'workwear', Marks & Spencer's main competitors were the Co-ops, which, in 1938, were selling one-third of the total supply of women's and children's clothes, consisting mainly of staple items such as women's underwear and overalls.[26] But what set Marks & Spencer apart from the Co-ops was that as well as providing these basic ranges of working clothing, the company also sold ranges intended to offer *fashion* to the working-class customer. For example, in 1938 the company sold new designs in underwear such as French knickers alongside the decidedly less glamorous 'Directoire' knickers.

The sheer physical expansion of Marks & Spencer on the high street from the late 1920s is impressive: in the twelve-year-period between March 1927 and March 1939, the number of stores increased from 126 to 234. By the mid-1930s, Marks & Spencer was represented in every town of any considerable size throughout the country and was shaping the look of the high street.[27] Buying procedures were becoming increasingly centralised from the company's London head office. From the 1930s, the pursuit of quality became possible because of the company's innovation in technological and design processes.

Technology at Marks & Spencer

Fashion as we currently understand it would not exist without technological innovation; fabric and clothing technology have redefined and changed fashion. When the mass production and retailing of clothing began, technology – that is, everything from the development of new fabrics with easy-care qualities; fabric performance (e.g. durability; making fabrics waterproof as well as shrink-resistant); the provision of a garment-sizing and grading system; to colour coordination and standardisation – became key to ensuring uniform quality. In all of these areas, Marks & Spencer was an early pioneer and its reputation as a retailer of quality clothing from the 1930s was established by placing technology and design at the centre of its retailing philosophy. A textile laboratory, merchandise development department and design department were established in rapid succession in the 1930s.

To begin with, Marks & Spencer had a long tradition of supporting, and subscribing to, research institutes for the clothing industries; important too was its reappraisal of the traditional relationship the retailer had with the supplier. Cutting out the wholesaler and dealing directly with suppliers enabled Marks & Spencer to negotiate directly on price and quality – and later design (Chapter 7). When, in the late 1920s, Israel Sieff persuaded supplier Corah of Leicester to deal directly with Marks & Spencer, Sieff's motivation was not only to avoid the wholesaler and reduce costs but also to facilitate long production runs in order to increase overall profits. And if at least part of those profits were ploughed back into product development, clothing quality could be improved. The *St Michael* brand (registered in 1928) became a guarantee to the customer that any article that carried it had been subjected to strict methods of quality control at every stage in its manufacture. It thus became a hallmark of 'quality' as well as an effective marketing tool.

In 1935, Marks & Spencer took the unusual step of establishing its own in-house textile laboratory with the aim of improving the quality of fabrics, with company technologists then specifying to the manufacturers the fabric quality required.[28] In the textile laboratory fabrics were tested to determine their durability and how they washed (including colour fastness); between 1935 and 1939, no fewer than 9,000 such tests were carried out. The results showed that the qualities of fabric used for some of the core Marks & Spencer clothing ranges were uneven. This resulted in the establishment of the merchandise development department in 1936, which was put under the direction of Dr Eric Kann, the gifted industrial scientist and expert in textile technology, with the specific task of improving the quality of Marks & Spencer merchandise. 'Here', explains Israel Sieff, 'we tested for colour fastness and shrinkage, the character of yarns and dyeing processes, and probed into the problems of the production of textiles by modern mass-production methods.'[29] Considering high quality and good design to be interdependent, Dr Kann also had the idea of creating a separate design department.[30]

During the Second World War government-led initiatives – in particular clothes rationing and the Utility clothing scheme – helped break down further existing class divisions in the consumption of clothing. Clothes rationing was formally introduced in 1941 and lasted until 1949. During this time, new clothing could only be bought with coupons and while the allowance was initially sixty-six coupons a year in spring 1942, this was reduced to sixty for fifteen months (approximately forty-eight coupons a year) due to increasing shortages.[31] Irrespective of income level, and unless you were able to get hold of coupons via the 'black market' (which some people did) the result was that the acquisition of clothing was limited by a fixed number of clothing coupons per year for all income brackets. In his 1969 *Concise History of Fashion*, James Laver based his assertion that 'any costume distinction between the classes disappeared' on the impact of clothes rationing and the Utility scheme.[32]

Conceived in 1941, the Utility clothing scheme meanwhile was launched the following year by Sir Laurence Watkinson who was at the Board of Trade in the period 1931–46. Like rationing, it was the result of wartime shortages, and a series of 'Clothes Restrictions Orders' regulated the amount of fabric used for garments and limited unnecessary trimmings, buttons and so on. At the same time, in July 1942, the Concentration Scheme limited the number of factories designated for clothing manufacture. Although the original Utility garments were designed by well-known couturiers under the pseudonym 'Incorporated Society of London Fashion Designers' (ISLFD), Utility clothing was subsequently made at every price level, from couture to mail order.[33] Based as they were on designer prototypes (each member of the ISLFD was asked to submit four basic specified outfits – top-coat, suit, afternoon dress and cotton overall dress) but produced at different price levels, Utility clothing theoretically gave everyone access to well-designed clothes. One effect of the Utility scheme and of clothes rationing was to encourage customers to be more discriminating in their choice of clothes by demanding better quality, more hard-wearing garments. Equally, manufacturers probably took more care in their choice of materials and paid more attention to their standards of garment make-up. Attempts at sizing standardisation contributed to the developing ready-made clothing industry.[34] Historians argue that, as a result, good design came within the reach of all.[35] Meanwhile, in October 1942, *Vogue* proclaimed the Utility scheme to be 'an outstanding example of applied democracy'. However, Laver's claim that class distinction disappeared must be an exaggeration given that the Utility scheme only ever affected 85 per cent of all cloth manufactured and the remaining 15 per cent could be made into non-Utility clothing, while wealthy women still had a stock of clothing on which to draw left over from the time before various war-time restrictions. On 8 December 1941 unmarried women (or childless widows) aged between twenty and thirty were conscripted and soon afterwards nineteen-year-olds as well; uniforms for the poor were quite shabby while richer women bought from the best London stores.[36] Meanwhile, the government's 'Make Do and Mend' campaign probably had more impact on the well-off, who had never out of sheer necessity needed to prolong a garment's life by mending it, though they may have done so for reasons of economy or sentimentality.

Despite disruption caused by wartime staff and goods shortages, the bombing of stores and consequent decline in turnover and profits, the retailing of Utility clothing by large retailers such as Marks & Spencer further contributed to the process of class levelling which the availability of ready-to-wear clothing had begun. Although class differences persisted, it became unfashionable at this time to look wealthy.[37] And because of rationing, people had to make clothes last – hardly a new challenge for poor families – so there was an incentive for the few clothes they did buy to be chosen for their quality and value. This factor, allied with the 'fashion' for a style that had less to do with looking opulent than maintaining a smart appearance with the minimum of effort, must have given the clothes being sold by Marks & Spencer a greater appeal.

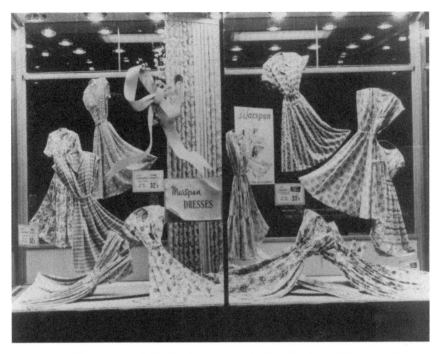

Figure 6.2 Photograph of Marks & Spencer window display of Marspun dresses, 1955. Catalogue no. P1/1/114/11 (courtesy of the M&S Company Archive, University of Leeds).

Utility clothes contributed to the greater part of Marks & Spencer's turnover during this period.[38] A large number of Marks & Spencer Utility-specification garments survive – with the familiar CC41 (Civilian Clothing 1941) label – including rayon *St Michael* Utility stockings and a man's shirt as well as a Utility housecoat with the *St Margaret* label (attached to those garments made by Corah of Leicester). The specifications for the manufacture of clothing under the Utility scheme drew widely on Marks & Spencer's knowledge and experience.[39] Marks & Spencer technologists cooperated with government scientists in devising Utility specifications. Paul Bookbinder explains how, in 1941, many of the standards formulated by Marks & Spencer during the 1930s for basic clothing materials, trimmings and garment manufacture were utilised by the government, with Marks & Spencer playing an important role in assisting the Board of Trade in determining standards for Utility clothing.[40] One such Utility fabric was a spun viscose later known as Marspun, which was a staple fabric used for Marks & Spencer dresses (Figure 6.2).

Therefore, in spite of short-term disruption, the effects of war on both the clothing industry as a whole, and on Marks & Spencer clothing in particular, were to contribute much to the democratisation of fashion in the longer term. The war accelerated scientific and technological progress in the textile and clothing industries. In 1943 Simon Marks set up a merchandising development research committee at Marks & Spencer, to assist in planning for post-war development by keeping abreast of scientific and technical developments in industry and agriculture.[41] By 1945 the merchandise development department was publishing a series of bulletins, which looked prophetically to the future: 'Trade papers carry stories of the wonders of nylon, plastics and all the other materials which may revolutionize our lives.'[42]

In post-war Britain, higher quality standards for clothing were established, including the principle of colour standardisation – colour, according to technologist Ismar Glasman, being 'the most important factor in promoting sales'.[43] Due to the scale of mass production required by the early 1950s, the same or matching garments could be manufactured across different suppliers. Consequently, colour standardisation (i.e. specified standards and tolerances of colour shades to which suppliers/dyers must adhere) became an important factor. It meant that such 'mix and match' ranges of jerseywear that became so popular at this time could be colour co-ordinated, and it paved the way for the sale of men's and women's suits from the 1970s and 1980s where exact colour matching would be essential.

Development of new and easy-care fabrics

Over time the negative impact on the environment as a consequence of the expansion of both the cotton and, later, the man-made/artificial and synthetic fibres industries has become more apparent as a result of growing world populations and the advent of 'fast fashion' (see Conclusion), but these industries have also made an enormous difference to people's lives globally, initially, at least, improving the standard of life of millions. In Britain Samuel Courtauld & Company started manufacturing viscose rayon in 1905, made with raw materials such as wood pulp, caustic soda, carbon disulfide and sulfuric acid which were relatively cheap and readily available. By 1925 not only Britain, but France, Germany, Holland, Italy, Japan and the United States were all significant producers of man-made/artificial fibres. The falling cost of rayon between 1921 and 1939, its suitability for blending with other fibres and continually improving performance made it attractive to the ready-to-wear industry, and it offered men and women on modest incomes an opportunity to enjoy mainstream fashions at affordable prices. Even a cursory look at the garments in the Marks & Spencer Company Archive reveals that rayon became an important fabric from the 1920s.

Not only did new fabrics create the potential for clothing to become cheaper and more accessible to working-class people, but from the 1950s many of the new fabrics were invested with easy-care qualities, thus making the burden of women's household drudgery lighter. Furthermore, fabrics using high performance (e.g. stretch) materials such as Lycra have made clothing more comfortable, not only for sport and leisure but for every-day, informal clothing such as jeans. Lycra was first introduced at Marks & Spencer in the early 1960s for use in corsetry but by the late 1990s was incorporated in one-quarter of all Marks & Spencer's clothing sales.[44] Indeed Lycra became an essential component of hosiery (Figure 6.3). In the period after the Second World War, Marks & Spencer technologists were preoccupied with introducing new, commercially viable fabrics as population increased and living standards slowly began to improve following the economic dislocation caused by the war. Natural fabrics such as cotton, linen and wool – though in high demand – were exhaustible and the perceived advantages of man-made and synthetic alternatives lay in their lower price potential and easy-care qualities. At the company's annual general meeting in 1964, Simon Marks reported that more than half of Marks & Spencer's textile sales were now in garments made from man-made and synthetic fibres. Including blends (with natural fabrics) the proportion was nearly two-thirds.[45] Marks & Spencer aspired to be at the cutting edge of these new developments. In a paper presented to the Textile Technology Symposium in 1969, textile technologist Ismar Glasman described how, 'through our technological strength, we [Marks & Spencer] were able to introduce these fabrics [the nylons and the acrylics] into our merchandise at a far greater pace than anybody else'.[46]

The discovery of nylon by Wallace Carothers (1896–1937) was announced by Du Pont in 1938 and this heralded the second generation of man-made

TIGHTS WITH
LYCRA*

MARKS & SPENCER

Figure 6.3 Marks & Spencer marketing leaflet for tights with Lycra, 1995. Catalogue no. HO/11/1/5/5 (courtesy of the M&S Company Archive, University of Leeds).

fibres. However, wartime scarcity meant that even when nylon appeared in Britain after 1945, there were signs in shop windows saying: 'Only available to foreign visitors.'[47] In an article for *St Michael News*, Marks & Spencer described how S. & J. Deyong Ltd (suppliers since 1934) obtained the first available supplies of warp-knitted nylon after the Second World War, producing nylon

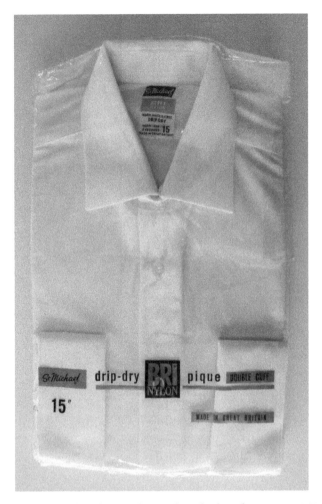

Figure 6.4 Men's Bri-Nylon shirt marketing drip-dry laundering, *ca.* 1965. Catalogue no. T11/10 (courtesy of the M&S Company Archive, University of Leeds).

waist slips for the retailer.[48] Nylon stockings were also sold by the company shortly after the war (*ca.* 1947) and a large range of nylon lingerie followed. By the late 1950s the company was selling nylon goods produced by British Nylon Spinners (Figure 6.4), who in 1958 introduced its own brand name Bri-Nylon.[49] The easy-care qualities of nylon were highlighted by Marks & Spencer in an article in *St Michael News* in 1960:

> Today, a girl simply takes a handful of detergent in the bowl, whisks the whole lot – slip, nightdress, briefs, bra and girdle – through the suds, gives

them one rinse and lets them drip-dry. That's the drill in millions of homes where there's St Michael Bri-Nylon lingerie.[50]

Orlon, originally known as 'Fibre A', was another of Du Pont's 'easy-living fibres' and was first announced in 1949.[51] With its remarkable capacity to form a staple fibre, thereby creating the bulkiness of wool, Orlon uniforms were described in the *Du Pont Magazine* in 1952 and this acrylic fabric was sold six years later at Marks & Spencer. Meanwhile, Courtelle was the first British acrylic fibre; it was produced by Courtaulds, introduced in the mid-1950s and trialled by Marks & Spencer in 1960. Since its introduction to the Marks & Spencer customer in about 1954 (following the lifting of British clothing restrictions in 1952), one of the most successful of the synthetic fabrics both for Marks & Spencer and for clothing retailers in general was/is polyester. The first public announcement of ICI's brand Terylene was placed in the *Manchester Guardian* on 5 October 1946. Along with Du Pont's Dacron, this fabric would soon command vast world markets.[52] 'Crease resisting', washable, permanently pleated 'sun-ray' skirts made of Terylene (sometimes mixed with wool) and Terylene trousers for men combined easy-care qualities with smart, popular fashion. The popularity of Crimplene – sold at Marks & Spencer by the mid-1960s – was short-lived. Although, as Susannah Handley points out, many people took it to be a completely new fabric, it was actually another form of polyester developed by ICI in 1955. What was different about it was the fact that it had been 'crimped'.[53] The man-made fibre triacetate (better known as Tricel) was marketed both by Courtaulds and British Celanese. Although acetate was first invented in 1914, technical problems held up its use until the 1950s.[54] At Marks & Spencer, it was sold as blouses from about 1957.

In the early years of their development, the new man-made and synthetic fibres were considered primarily as 'substitutes' for natural fibres, invested with little aesthetic value. By the early 1960s, however, they were becoming important in their own right, providing the customer with what was perceived as a better product in terms of performance, colour and, significantly, price. Until the late 1960s, garments made from synthetic fibres were generally more expensive than cotton and the more established man-made fibres such as rayon, and therefore gave a better return per square foot of selling space.[55] In 1971, an analysis of sales by fibre revealed that whereas sales of natural fabrics had increased from £62,440,000 in 1966 to £73,175,000 in 1970, sales of man-made and synthetic fabrics (nylon; polyesters; acrylics and rayons) had risen from £116,100,000 to £191,025,000 in the same period.[56] Simon Marks made it known that he wanted clothes bought at Marks & Spencer to make women's lives easier: 'Not only do they [nylon, Orlon, Terylene and Tricel] provide attractive garments, but they also have the advantage of easing the housewife's daily burden.'[57] As a result, 'increasingly too it [St Michael] is becoming a symbol of easier living … The lot of many a housewife has been lightened by St Michael drip-dry and easy to launder garments'.[58]

Hand in hand with the development of easy-care fabrics went the availability and consumption of labour-saving devices for the home. Historian Elizabeth Roberts observes that to have an electric iron in the home was usual by 1960, while 3.6 per cent of families nationally had washing machines in 1942, compared with 64 per cent by 1969.[59] However, the arrival of the latter did not necessarily mean that women spent less time on domestic chores.[60] Mass Observation, for example, reported in 1961 that suburban London housewives spent a staggering seventy-one hours per week on domestic activities.[61] In spite of the undisputed enthusiasm in the post-war period for man-made and synthetic fabrics and their easy-care qualities, they did not replace natural fabrics. In fact, in the 1950s, when British cotton firms were being hit by foreign competition and exports were declining, Marks & Spencer aimed to promote the cotton industry by highlighting the fact that 99 per cent of the cotton cloth sold in Marks & Spencer stores was spun, woven and finished in Britain.[62] Even as Marks & Spencer was concentrating on the development of the new synthetics, the company also focused its technological expertise on giving natural fabrics easy-care qualities.

Of these developments, one of the most important was that of machine-washable wool. From the early 1950s, *St Michael* knitwear was made shrink-resistant so that it could be safely washed by hand.[63] The development of machine-washable wool would of course depend on this innovation. By the mid-1960s, a two-ply yarn for a harder-wearing fabric and the application of a special shrink-resist treatment made lambswool and Shetland wool increasingly popular for men's and women's knitwear. The development of machine-washable botany wool was followed closely by the announcement of Marks & Spencer's first machine-washable lambswool and Shetland wool garments in 1972.

While synthetics such as acrylic, nylon, polyester and Lycra were here to stay, there was a resurgence in the popularity of natural fabrics from the late 1980s and 1990s, marketed for their luxurious feel and appearance. Once again, the emphasis was on giving them easy-care qualities such as machine-washable silk. The success of non-iron cotton, first in menswear and then in the late 1990s in womenswear, also reflected the increasing demand for fabrics with the aesthetic qualities of natural fabrics but requiring the minimum of care. Likewise, the appearance in 1987 in menswear of machine-washable suits (70 per cent polyester and 30 per cent wool, with a polyester lining)[64] and then in womenswear in the mid-1990s was an indication of changing lifestyles and of the increasing demands made upon men and women in juggling work and domestic roles.

Marks & Spencer technologists aimed continually to improve the quality of fabric and garment performance. In the early 1960s, for example, the company announced a 'revolutionary new treatment for rainwear' called Scotchguard, enabling rainwear to be dry-cleaned without damaging the proofing.[65] Then in the late 1970s and early 1980s, the company strove to improve the extent to which its range of adult rainwear was waterproof, following tests conducted by the 'rain simulator' in the textile laboratory which revealed that water was penetrating the seams of garments as a result of the type of sewing thread used. Colourfastness (colours that do not run when washed or wet) also became an important element in establishing the company's reputation for quality as it aimed to match or exceed the highest standards laid down by the industry. For example, in the late 1960s, Marks & Spencer introduced a new standard on *St Michael* nylon underwear fabrics: approximately thirty different shades were colourfast when washed at 60°C. A writer for *St Michael News* explained: 'That is about ten degrees warmer than anyone would want to wash nylon at ... This raises the standard to ISO3, the highest practical standard for washing nylon issued by the International Standards Organization.'[66] In addition, the quality of merchandise was monitored both at the point of manufacture as well as in stores.

Establishing a reliable sizing system was key to the success of the ready-to-wear clothing industry in Britain. From the late 1920s, more sophisticated American sizing methods were used by companies producing ready-made clothing. For example, Olive O'Neill, designer for the high-quality ready-to-wear company Dorville, dissatisfied with the existing British standards of manufacture and, above all, sizing, adopted American methods of sizing, grading and manufacture in the 1930s.[67] Marks & Spencer also adopted American sizing as the prototype for its grading system.[68] From the 1950s, however, the company conducted a number of size surveys, initially for staple ranges such as women's stockings, in the quest for a more scientific approach to this complex issue. Their sizing for women (other than for stockings) was based largely upon a survey conducted by the Board of Trade in 1951. But by the 1980s, it became clear that the height and body curves of women had changed over the preceding thirty years, due to such factors as the keep-fit boom, different nutrition, the contraceptive pill and the casting aside of body-shaping underwear. In 1988 a survey was undertaken in association with Loughborough University and with the participation of ten Marks & Spencer suppliers, involving more than 6,000 women aged between seventeen and sixty-nine, at thirty-one stores. The results were published in 1989 and revealed that the 'average' British woman was 1.62 m (5 ft 4 inches) tall, that is, 2.5 cm (1 inch) taller than thirty years previously. As a result of the survey, a more generous size 10 was introduced, so enabling the company to bring in what it described as a 'meaningful size 8'.[69] The first major size survey for men was undertaken in 1984, and for boys in 1979, the latter also in association with Loughborough University. There was less urgency for girls because of standards laid down by BS 3728, which was based on a survey done in the United States before the Second World War, marginally updated in the mid-1960s. In fact, it was not until 1986 that a major survey for girls was carried out.

In August 1996, *Draper's Record* reported that Loughborough University was again working with Marks & Spencer and its suppliers on sizing research. The university survey involved 200 adult women and looked mainly at bra sizes. While the surveys of the 1980s had used traditional methods, the 1996 project team used the 'Loughborough Anthropometric Body Scanner'. The article describes how the scanner shines across the body while it rotates, taking coordinates for the whole body in eleven minutes. The shape is then entered into the computer for use in CAD (computer-aided design) programs and manufacturing. This initiated widespread research into sizing within the retail industry including that carried out by the Burton Group and Oasis.[70]

The cumulative effect of technological innovation on the way in which clothing is both (mass) produced and consumed has been to push the boundaries that define fashion. Not everyone, however, saw the extension of cheap 'fashion' to working-class people as a 'good' thing. Philip Larkin's 1961 poem 'The Large Cool Store', 'selling cheap clothes / Set out in simple sizes plainly / (Knitwear, Summer Casuals, Hose, / In browns and greys, maroon and navy)', if not about Marks & Spencer per se, is about the (negative) impact that democratisation had on individuality and the *look* of clothing, whether hanging in the store or worn on the body. It can be read as an indictment of the erosion of taste and of the way in which cheap high-street clothing produced dull uniformity, reflecting the lives of those 'Who leave at dawn low terraced houses / Timed for factory, yard and site'[71], reducing everything to the 'weekday world' described in the first and second stanzas of the poem.

While trends towards democratisation described in this chapter resulted in a redrawing of the lines that linked class with particular fabrics and styles, what, we should now ask, has been the role of the designer in all this? How has high-end designer clothing maintained its hold in an environment in which quality garments can be bought at a fraction of its price? While 'designer' fashion may still be beyond the reach of many, designers have made huge adjustments in order to make their clothing available to a wider market. They have done this by introducing ready-to-wear ranges, being open to being copied and designing directly for the high street. They have also made the exclusivity of the 'designer product' obtainable by creating perfume, the 'affordable signature of the designer which reaches a wider international market'.[72]

In the last decades of the twentieth century, some high-street retailers re-negotiated their relationships with designers with the result that fashion has become less a statement of class or financial status than a reflection of age, ethnicity, religion, gender, culture and taste. Meanwhile the 'zoning' of shopping areas means that there are now many markets as a result of the democratisation processes described in this chapter. Today, for example, in a relatively small area of London W1 can be found the department stores and relatively low-priced chains of Oxford and Regent Street, the bespoke tailoring trade of Savile Row, luxury brands in Bond Street and, slightly further east, the skate brands such as Palace and Supreme, where the queues just to enter these niche shops seem to fly in the face of the move towards democratisation. In a way they are the antithesis of what we understand as democratisation because it is not necessarily class or financial status that will get us into these shops, but rather *time*.

7

Design and class

With the changes in social structures that have taken place since the late eighteenth century resulting from, and reflected in, revolution, war, technological innovation and developments in retailing, the threads that linked rank/status and later class with fashion became intertwined, and it can be difficult to unravel these diverse strands. As the high street expanded and offered all social groups affordable clothing that could be put together effortlessly, the time spent in making or coordinating the detail of fashion and accessories was eroded. That is not to say that today we have any less time than our parents and grandparents did, but rather that we seem to prefer to spend the time *shopping* for, rather than making, clothes. And the development of the high street with its diversity of clothing, accessory and footwear retailers has enabled us to do this. The result is that the ubiquity of high-street fashion while, on the one hand, apparently offering more choice has, on the other hand, lulled us into what is arguably a dull uniformity and standardisation. Nevertheless, the cache of good design and exclusiveness is still very much a part of desirable living and culture. And in the second decade of the twenty-first century, we seem to hear more about the demise of the high street than we do about the waning of the importance of *design*.

It may be true that the actual number of couture customers is relatively small. However, diffusion lines, designer 'spin-offs' resulting from trends from catwalk shows of the fashion weeks of the European capitals impacting both ready-to-wear and high-street fashion, as well as the sales of designer jeans, handbags and perfume, together have an enormous influence; for example, the designer signature reaches a wider international market as the result of the sales of (affordable) perfume.[1] And then there is the direct impact of designer and luxury brands that have become highly desirable, if not always accessible. So, for example, if a whole designer outfit may be out of the reach of the majority of people, a classic or statement Chanel, Hermès or Prada handbag, while costing anything from £1,000 upwards, may be considered worth investing in both for its quality and design. (Prada, for example, operates a free repairs service for the lifetime of the bag.) But the success of cheaper, 'middle-range' handbags, such as the Michael Kors label – which appear to offer some of the qualities of a Prada bag – bears testimony to the ways in which high-end design still influences mass-produced, inferior 'versions'. Influences can go in the other direction too with trends working their way up from 'street' level: cotton jeans, for example, over the course of the twentieth century, changed their status as humble workwear to fashion garments synonymous with youth.

In 1976 the Italian jeans company Fiorucci opened its first New York jeans store and it instantly became a social hub.[2] Prewashing of denim and abrading denim physically weakens the material but the weakness adds to the perceived value of the textile, 'a complete reversal of traditional clothing values', observes Emma McClendon.[3] According to Jennifer Craik, jeans have become a 'symbol of middle-class revolt from the strictures of respectability and conformity', while also having been taken up successfully by designer labels, with sales of Calvin Klein jeans reaching about $400 million worldwide in 1984.[4] 'Once a stigmatised marker of social class', jeans, argues McClendon, are now 'an accepted basic of everyday clothing', and have 'transitioned into high fashion'.[5] According to Ted Polhemus, 'Jeans have become the most ubiquitous street style garment' (Figure 7.1).[6]

In Chapters 5 and 6, my focus was on the way in which fashion was democratised as a consequence of the development of the ready-to-wear clothing industry, the products of which were then marketed and sold by high-street retailers (who, in the case of Marks & Spencer, also worked with fabric and garment suppliers to develop increasingly sophisticated fabric and clothing technologies), with the result that long-held prejudices against ready-made clothing were cast aside. This chapter will begin with a brief summary of some key moments in the history of design/couture in relation to class, followed by a discussion of the role of design on the high street, including a 'postscript' to the theme already begun in Chapter 6 about the way Marks & Spencer offered the customer well-designed products at affordable, non-'designer' prices. Over the years their approach – adopted by other retailers – has resulted in divergent

Figure 7.1 Model Dylan Xue wears an Yves Saint Laurent bag, Fendi sunglasses, Miu Miu shoes, vintage top and jeans on day 4 of London Women's Fashion Week, spring/summer 2016, on 19 September 2016 in London, England (photo by Kirstin Sinclair/Getty Images Entertainment).

critiques of this aspect of the democratisation of fashion: on the one hand, the company was praised for making good design accessible to working- and middle-class people. (This then raised questions about the 'ethics' of selling clothing and accessories at the much higher prices asked by designers.) On the other hand, the company was accused of plagiarising the designs of others and of 'watering down' the design input of clothing generally. Following the emergence of youth and popular fashion from the 1950s and 1960s, alternative visions of designer 'fashion' – offered in particular by Japanese designers emerging in the 1970s and the Belgian 'deconstructionists' in the 1980s and 1990s – questioned the correlation between design and the traditional role of couture and their respective relationships with class. Our clothing changes how we perceive ourselves and our bodies and should make us feel 'good', but what 'good' means has altered over time and is affected by changes in social structures and the cultural (re)positioning described in previous chapters.

Couture

In the past, the emphasis on the role of the couturier (or, in the case of Rose Bertin, the 'marchande des modes') in influencing changes in fashion reflects not only the way in which the history of fashion as an academic discipline has focused on the dress of the elite and the upper classes but also the ways in which trends in historiography looked to the 'great man' or, less frequently, the 'great woman' as being the key influence(s) on major shifts in fashion. The history of couture has been well-documented and has privileged an approach to fashionable change which views the designer as the great arbiter and prime mover of fashion. Suffice it to say here that since the late eighteenth century when Rose Bertin created her 'confections' for Queen Marie Antoinette (Chapter 2), the role of the designer has changed over time. However, what did not change until the middle decades of the twentieth century was the direct association that couture fashion – made to fit the particular person who bought it – had with money, status and class. This was quite simply because the clothes were both beyond the means of working-class people and the tulle and lace creations of the person who is often described as the 'inventor' of haute couture, Charles Frederick Worth (1825–1895), were only appropriate to the then *lifestyles* of royalty and leisured high society. So even if she could have afforded to dress in high fashion, it is hard to imagine a Victorian working-class woman working on the pit-brow in Wigan or in a Manchester cotton factory wearing a crinoline or a bustle, the popularisation of the latter often attributed to Worth. Notwithstanding the fact that much has changed since the time of Worth – Kate Middleton, the Duchess of Cornwall, dressed in Ted Baker clothing is a far cry from Princess Metternich or Empress Eugénie in Worth gowns – even into the twentieth century, the restrictive clothes designed by Paul Poiret (1879–1944) and the liberating 'chitons' in sumptuous pleated silk by Mariano Fortuny (1871–1949) – very different though they were from what had gone before – catered to the rich.

The First World War and its aftermath, along with associated social change including the increasingly significant role of women in the workplace, affected female fashion and its relationship with class: into the 1920s not only did looser styles become the norm, but sportswear began to influence mainstream fashion. In 1925 the French designer Jean Patou (1880–1936) opened a series of rooms on the ground floor of 7, rue Saint-Florentin, Paris, which he called his 'Coin des Sports'. Over a decade before this, however, Gabrielle (Coco) Chanel (1883–1971) had opened a shop selling what could be described as the first ever line of women's 'sportswear' in soft and comfortable wool-jersey in the bathing and gambling resort of Deauville in 1913. Not only did the styles originated by Chanel have a profound effect on women's attitudes to their clothing from the 1920s and 1930s – *comfort* could be combined with glamour – but they translated into clothes that could be copied easily and disseminated widely and that could, therefore, be described as classless. How many times have we seen versions of the 'Chanel' boxy jacket and straight skirt made of tweed-like fabric with large gilt buttons sold on the high street, or the repeated reproduction of the 'little black dress'? Or, indeed, the quilted bag of leather, plastic or fabric with a gilt shoulder chain? Chanel seemed to be unperturbed about being copied, believing that clothing only transformed itself into fashion when it filtered down to, and was known on, the high street. The irony is that imitation has in fact increased the popularity of the original, with the classic Chanel 'quilted' leather bag retailing at over £3,000 in 2018, while older versions retain their value as vintage items. Perhaps the success of the Chanel 'label' can be ascribed in part to the fact that Chanel designs lend themselves easily to imitation (Figures 7.2 and 7.3).

Following the scarcity of clothing during the Second World War, the work of Christian Dior (1905–1957) and especially his 'corolle' line, christened the New Look, took fashion by storm when it was launched in spring 1947 with its full skirt, nipped-in waist and padded bust and hips, reminiscent of pre–First World War styles. Interesting though the debates surrounding the New Look are – for example, the idea that it was not really 'new' but followed logically from the fashionable line that had been developing in the late 1930s that was

Figure 7.2 General view of the Chanel Haute Couture Fashion show, during Paris Fashion Week, spring/summer 2008, at Grand Palais, Paris, France, on 22 January 2008 (photo by Dominique Charriau/Wire Image/Getty Images).

Figure 7.3 Bag and shoes by fashion designer Gabrielle Chanel as part of the exhibition 'Fashion in France, 1947–1957' at the Palais Galliera, Paris, France, which ran 12 July to 2 November 2014. The photo was taken on 10 July 2014 (photo by Stephane de Sakutin/AFP/Getty Images).

abruptly ended by the war; or that it represented a 'plot' to wrest control of fashion back to Paris from the competition posed by the United States; or that it heralded cyclical fashion changing each season with a new theme or style – more pertinent here is the fact that, despite the controversy around the use of so much fabric at a time in Britain when clothing was still being rationed, it was easily and quickly translated into affordable, mainstream fashion. For example, the pages of *St Michael News* illustrate the Marks & Spencer version(s) while the successful ready-to-wear company Deréta produced a grey flannel 'New Look' suit soon after the news of Christian Dior's collection, with seven hundred sold in a West End store within two weeks.[7] Moreover, Elizabeth Ewing argues that the New Look ushered in a period when fashion became available to everyone,[8] while 'Make Do and Mend' came into its own, with women sewing extra rings around the hems of their skirts to make them fuller and longer.

Yves Henri Donat Matthieu Saint Laurent (known as Yves Saint Laurent) (1936–2008) worked for Dior before branching out on his own and opening his own fashion house in 1961. Like Chanel, he intuited the mood of the time and was an astute observer of what was going on around him. The stuffiness

Figure 7.4 Fashion designer Yves Saint Laurent and his associate Betty Saint (aka Betty Catroux) wearing sunglasses, printed shirts, jeans and boots and sitting on the grass in Central Park, New York. *Vogue*, 1968 (photo by Maurice Hogenboom/Condé Nast via Getty Images).

of couture – the manner in which it had perpetuated the close association between fashion and class – had already been partly dispelled by Chanel but Yves Saint Laurent put the final nail in the coffin (Figure 7.4). His ready-to-wear collections reflected what was happening at (edgy) street level and his clothes aimed to cross the divides between couture, ready-to-wear and the high street, specifically the 'high street' of the Parisian Left Bank. He was the first living fashion designer to have a major retrospective devoted to him (at the Costume Institute of the Metropolitan Museum of Art in 1983); this was followed by many exhibitions of his work throughout the world, including in such places as Beijing, Paris, Moscow, Saint Petersburg, Sydney, Tokyo and Marseille.

Design on the high street

What was the relationship between design and its 'interpretation' on the high street in the seventy-or-so years after the high-street chains came into their own from the 1930s? Returning to a focus on Marks & Spencer, in the wake of pioneering a textile laboratory in 1935 (Chapter 6), a year later the company established a design department – both developments the brainchild of Dr Eric Kann – reflecting the company's mission to keep abreast of the latest trends in fashion, in particular to have oversight of the styling, colour and fabric of the clothing manufactured by suppliers and sold in stores. In these early days, the function of the design department was practical with in-house designers employed to do pattern-cutting and make up samples; as time passed a more interpretative role dominated, which included translating current fashion trends into wearable fashion appropriate to the company's customers. In the 1980s the design department introduced a 'design brief', which drew on information proffered by the fashion prediction agencies such as Trend Union headed by Lidewij Edelkoort, reflecting the way in which high-street fashion assimilated major social, cultural and fashion trends including styling, fabric and colour.

The involvement by Marks & Spencer in the working out of the Board of Trade's Utility clothing scheme evidences the inspiration and impact of good design. A formative influence in the post–Second World War period was Hans Schneider who headed up the Design Department, having joined the company in 1949. Always keeping abreast of design developments on the Continent generally, and on Parisian couture specifically, Schneider made it his mission to improve the design input of the clothing ranges by visiting trade fairs, travelling with technologists and selectors on trips to Europe in order to ensure that those fashions that were 'appropriate' (that is, not too fashionable!) were made into a reality for the Marks & Spencer customer. In the 1950s and 1960s the houses of Dior and Chanel provided much inspiration for ranges of women's dresses and suits, and former designer Richard Lachlan recalls going to the Dior couture shows in Paris in the 1960s and buying toiles to be used for Marks & Spencer designs.[9] In addition, Hans Schneider acknowledged the importance of Spanish designer Balenciaga as 'the leader in the great classic tradition' and Yves Saint Laurent for the 'boutique trends'.[10] In 1962 the couturier Michael of Carlos Place (whose work, likened to that of Balenciaga and known for its 'stylish tailoring and strong uncluttered design statements')[11] was appointed to work as a consultant for Marks & Spencer. This was the beginning of a tradition of employing consultants to act as 'constructive critics several times a year', when the Marks & Spencer inhouse teams (of designers and selectors) have put together designs for the coming season; the consultants helped to 'edit and advise on cloth, suggesting changes where necessary'.[12] However, even before Michael's employment, unpublished correspondence at the Marks & Spencer Company Archive reveal that Parisian designer Anny Blatt worked in a consultancy capacity for much of the 1950s in order to advise the company on the jerseywear and knitwear ranges.[13]

The establishment of the men's suit department in 1972 coincided with the employment of the Italian Angelo Vitucci as consultant in 1970. In the early 1990s Italian expertise was again enlisted for the new 'Italian Collections' as part of an overhaul of men's suits, in which Marks & Spencer worked closely with both the company's Italian and British manufacturers on design and tailoring.[14] (Many of the fabrics used by Marks & Spencer came from leading Italian manufacturer Marzotto, supplier for Giorgio Armani.[15]) In 1985 menswear designer Paul Smith was appointed as a consultant and he was followed by Bruce Oldfield, appointed two years later in 1987. Oldfield gave Marks & Spencer considerable prestige not least because he already designed clothes for members of the royal family, including Princess Diana. In this way, consultants thus seemed to be bridging the class divide between high-end design and the high street. In 1990, Betty Jackson (winner of the British Fashion Council's Designer of the Year Award in 1985) was first employed as womenswear consultant, helping Marks & Spencer to 'create classic ranges with a sharp fashion edge'.[16]

As a result of closer relationships between high street and designer, the question has often been asked about how relevant high-end fashion at the end of the twentieth century was to the clothes that most people wore? In 1997, fashion journalist Tamsin Blanchard pointed out that 'without designer level fashion, high-street fashion would have no impetus to move forward … no direction'.[17] Most notably the 1990s also saw the move by high-street retailers to sell ranges originated by well-known designers, an overt message to customers that fashion at the highest level was now available and accessible to them, eradicating, it seemed, any vestiges of *class* association with designer fashion. For example, in 1994, Tanya Sarne of the Ghost label – her hallmark was beautiful viscose dresses and separates cut on the bias – was asked to design a range of dresses for manufacture by Coats Viyella to be retailed by Marks & Spencer. The range was extremely successful and by 1997 Coats Viyella had deals with Marion Foale (for cardigan 'jackets') and Jeff Griffin (for menswear). 'Once upon a time, there was *fashion*, and there was *Fashion*. The two were very different ... the two were parallel universes', claimed journalist Harriet Lane in the *Observer*.[18] In other words, mass 'fashion' and couture and designer 'Fashion' were worlds away from each other. However, the development of ranges by high-profile designers for high-street stores made designer fashion accessible – akin to the development of diffusion lines – and continued to democratise fashion even though Ben de Lisi and Pearce Fionda admitted that the products they designed for the high street were not comparable to their most expensive clothing in terms of the 'intricacy in cut and attention to detail'.[19] In addition, the difference between, say, a designer garment and its high-street 'equivalent' – apart from the price tag – is often to be found in fabric, cut and the details such as buttons. Even so, as Roger Tredre observed in 1997, 'the relationship between the designer and the high street is undergoing a spectacular transformation'.[20] Other retailers were doing similar deals to those brokered between Marks & Spencer and its suppliers: for example, Dorothy Perkins employed designer duo Suzanne Clements and Ignacio Ribeiro, Debenhams employed Jasper Conran while BHS utilised the talent of Paul Frith. The 1990s, observed Lisa Grainger, was 'all about labels, and being fashionable means knowing your Dolce & Gabbana from your Gucci' but, on the other hand, 'who needs that one-off Jasper Conran dress when he is designing a similar one for Debenhams at a tenth of the price?'[21]

Moves to make the origination of a design crystal clear to the public came in the wake of ITV's *World in Action* documentary (15 January 1996) which focused on a number of cases in which Marks & Spencer was accused of copying the designs of others, namely, a Liza Bruce 'dip-dyed' swimsuit. Whatever the truth of the allegation, it was perhaps no coincidence that shortly before this programme was broadcast, fashion commentators had been praising Marks & Spencer for having apparently reinvented itself and for casting aside its association with 'populist fashion of the lowest common denominator' and for being on the 'fashion offensive' with 'not-quite-Joseph angora knits, near-Prada peacoats and hint-of-Hindmarch bags'.[22] Sally Brampton in her article 'The Adoration of St Michael', meanwhile, asserted that 'really fashionable women had begun to shop at Marks & Spencer'.[23] And following a line of 'supermodels' employed by the company to sell their clothing – beginning with Twiggy in the 1960s, Claudia Schiffer in 1990 and later Linda Evangelista who was photographed by Patrick Demarchelier wearing a black Marks & Spencer miniskirt, polo-neck and thigh-length socks – model Amber Valetta then appeared on the front cover of *Vogue* in May 1996 wearing a £21 Marks and Spencer polyester shantung shirt. This seemed to be an affirmation of the company's newfound status among the gurus of high fashion. At the same time – and despite the furore caused by the issues raised by the *World in Action* programme – newspapers were running regular columns in which a high-street (cheaper) version of an expensive high-end designer garment or a look that was 'on trend' was reviewed and compared, such as the *Observer* 'Copycats' feature in summer/autumn 1997. Furthermore, if clothing as cheap as the £21 Marks & Spencer shirt was being advertised by *Vogue* – the magazine that traditionally advertised and wrote about expensive, elite fashion – what did this say about 'traditional' relationships between class, wealth and status, and fashion? Had the demarcations linking clothing and fabric to particular classes become anomalous or even obsolete?

The cult of youth

The association between class and fashion shifted demonstrably in the decades following the Second World War. As we have seen, this was a gradual and evolutionary process that was as much the result of social change influencing customer demand as it was due to the impact of new technologies. Yet the two are so inextricably linked that it is often difficult to separate one from the other: changes in fashions both reflect and influence social change. The relaxation of austerity following war-time hardship and the post-war 'baby boom' years went hand in hand with the recognition of the power and optimism of youth as a new force in fashion along with the latter's quest for independence and new styles that were *not* necessarily based on adult fashion or perceived to reflect adult values. The United States was a barometer of this new mood and perhaps because the hierarchies of class that were bolstered by tradition were less ingrained there, youth culture – along with its questioning

Figure 7.5 Motorcycle gang in the film *The Wild One*: Johnny Strabler (Marlon Brando) and his gang stand together on the sidewalk (photographer not known; John Springer Collection/Corbis Historical via Getty Images).

of cultural 'norms' – emerged more rapidly here than in Britain. Directed by László Benedek and produced by Stanley Kramer, the 1953 film *The Wild One* is best remembered for Marlon Brando's sullen and unnerving rebelliousness in the role of Johnny Strabler. The image of Brando in a biker leather jacket became a cultural icon of the 1950s. Initially banned by the British Board of Film Censors, the film received an X certificate in 1967 and was first seen by the UK public in 1968 (Figure 7.5).

In London – and indeed across Britain as a whole – while the large high-street chains seemed unable to capture successfully the growing youth market (other than perhaps for basic underwear and hosiery), which included people who had merely heard about the hardships of the war from their parents but did not actually experience it, the late 1950s and 1960s were an exciting time for fashion. On the one hand, subcultural style and its associations with popular music began to influence mainstream trends; on the other hand, the opening of 'boutiques' such as Mary Quant in 1955 and Biba in 1966 heralded an innovative approach to fashion and styling – including hair and make-up – and with this, new means of disseminating the styles of the young, who might overturn accepted or traditional cultural codes in searching for their own identity, but who did not necessarily want to express either individuality or 'tribe' solidarity through some of the more 'extreme' looks adopted by subcultures such as mods, goths, hippies and punks. The popularity of these boutiques highlighted the failure of more mainstream retailers of mass fashion such as Marks & Spencer to capture the youth and teen market as much as they demonstrated the way in which the market was changing with its 'invention' of the teenager in the mid-1950s. A new wave of high-street stores that were aimed primarily at the youth market appeared: Topshop (founded 1964) (and later Topman in 1978), Miss Selfridge (founded in 1966), New Look (founded in 1969), Primark (first opened in Dublin in 1969 under the name Penneys), followed later by H&M which opened its first store in the United Kingdom in 1976. Meanwhile, Harriet Quick, writing for the *Guardian*, stated in 1995 that 'the British high street is unique'. Making special mention of Topshop, she added that 'in no other country is there such a choice of cheap high fashion and nowhere else do these fashion stores play such an integral part in the rite of passage of teenage girls'.[24] In an article in the *Times* in 1995, the controversial journalist A. A. Gill argued that whereas in the past, men and women dressed 'hierarchically', the burgeoning 'choice and cheapness of clothes' had led to a trend towards 'come-as-you-areism' in which the cult of health and youth were paramount:

> A generation ago there was no such thing as teenage fashion – there was no such thing as a teenager. You went straight from shorts into a cut-down version of what your parents wore, and wore it until you were buried in it. Now fashion is driven by youth and fitness. We are teenagers from six to sixty. Casual clothes are sporty, they imply physical ability. Trainers, t-shirts, tracksuits, tennis shirts and baseball caps are the universal uniform. American presidents, God help them, have themselves photographed in shorts.[25]

The expansion of universities in Britain and political shifts towards social inclusion within higher education alongside the growth of the importance of popular music all gave a new impetus to fashion where class became less significant as a factor in defining or determining it. Writing in the *Spectator*, Arthur House looked back to 1988–9 and the end of a decade marked by social division and unemployment. He describes how British youth culture had undergone 'the biggest revolution since the 1960s': the music was acid house and the drug, ecstasy, and together, he writes, they created the 'second summer of love', a 'euphoric high that lasted a year and a half and engulfed Britain's youth in a hedonistic haze of peace, love and unity'. Acid house, he observed, 'transcended class and race, town and country, north and south'.[26] While the impact of this extraordinary fusion between music and popular culture – including fashion – may have been exaggerated by House (and in any case it did not last), it certainly influenced the way that relationships between fashion and class evolved in the 1990s, often in response to music and the festival 'scene'. By the 1990s some fashion journalists went as far as to describe music festivals as *the* influence on fashion. Marion Hume claimed: 'Last week, the Glastonbury festival took over from the King's Road, from Carnaby Street of old, and from the London designer fashion scene as *the* place to be.'[27]

Anti-consumerist tendencies born out of capitalist and Thatcherite models were definitely here to stay and the realisation that we mostly all had too many 'cheap' clothes destined for landfill after a couple of seasons' wear raised questions about the sustainability of a fashion industry that was built on the supply of constantly changing styles. The last decade of the twentieth century has sometimes been described as a 'shapeless decade': a period of uncertainty about the direction in which fashion was heading as we approached the new millennium and in which the recycling both of actual clothing as well as of historical and vintage styles became the main 'trend'. Marion Hume commented on the return of punk after only a couple of decades since its first appearance.[28] In 1993 she also wrote about 'the new mood' in fashion: 'The whole world is changing. Globs of gold and short, sharp suits have ceded to bagginess, scruffiness, second-hand and ethnic clothes',[29] which, she observed, are even worn by top fashion editors. This was 'grunge' and it was worn by the new 'waif' models, Kate Moss, Emma Balfour and Cecilia Chancellor, whose looks were in sharp contrast to that of the 'supermodels' of the 1980s and early 1990s.

'Grunge' was defined in the *Guardian* as both a 'style of rock music originating in the U.S. in the late 1980s, featuring a distorted guitar sound' and a 'deliberately untidy and uncoordinated fashion style'.[30] Reporting on the grunge phenomenon, Roger Tredre traces its origins to Seattle, where students in the late 1980s tuned into a local radio station, KCMU, that played demo tapes by local bands. The music was loud and guitar-based, 'low on melody but high on energy'.[31] By the beginning of the 1990s, the same local bands were attracting much greater attention: names such as Mudhoney, Soundgarden, Pearl Jam and Nirvana became international acts. Grunge developed into a 'mainstream cultural phenomenon, embracing music, fashion and the lifestyles of the twentysomething generation'.[32] British journalists observed that 'on this side of the Atlantic, grunge is not so very surprising to anyone young living on a tight budget' with the mixing of shapes and styles of clothing and footwear having been the 'basis of British street fashion for years', while in Paris, designers such as Martin Margiela and Jean Colonna had been preaching the virtues of flea market chic and inside-out fashion for several seasons.[33] Journalists pointed out the irony of the rapid assimilation of grunge by the film and fashion worlds, given that in its early stages grunge was 'anti-fashion and anything but mainstream'.[34] Journalist Suzanne Moore had a more cynical 'interpretation':

> Baggy jumpers, messed-up hair, clothes that have shrunk and faded in the wash, scruffy old boots, this is apparently now the look to aspire to. This look we have been told started in Seattle a couple of years ago (funny, I remember seeing it in every student town in England 10 years ago), inspired by bands such as Nirvana. Straining for sociological significance, this style we have been informed is a sign of anti-consumerist times, of recession and depression. Let's not mention designer desperation.[35]

Fashion commentators were also critical of the ways in which designers of the 1980s and 1990s who 'invented' deconstruction adopted ideas and motifs that already existed among the young both on the high street and in youth gatherings, upgrading them to become high fashion. Suzanne Moore was vehement in her criticism of this trend:

> Taking cues from designers and then adapting them for everyday living seems perfectly sensible. What I cannot abide is when it works the other

way round – when designers take something off the street and then claim to have invented it.[36]

What Suzanne Moore – who was not writing from the perspective of a *fashion* journalist – and other commentators were doing was picking up on influences on mainstream fashion that had little to do with the elite world of couture. What she described as 'designer desperation' – designers taking influences from the street which they then claimed to have invented – was also an indication of the increasing disassociation between class and fashion.

Deconstruction: the challenge of Japan and Belgium

Since at least the time of Charles Frederick Worth's residence there, Paris was considered by many to be the centre of haute couture. However, challenges to the hegemony of French fashion came from the United States in the post–Second World War period and then later from Japan and Italy. Japanese designers, in particular Issey Miyake (b. 1939), Kenzo Takada (b. 1939; opened his own shop Jungle Jap in 1970) and Yohji Yamamoto (b. 1943), had a huge influence from the 1970s onwards and posed a challenge to the way in which 'Western' fashion had evolved. Rather than being overly influenced by the past, Issey Miyake, from the time he presented his first collection in Paris in 1973, looked to and accepted the future in contrast to Western fashion with its unremitting focus on continuous change and its obsession with hierarchy, status and class as well as with the past (reviving and re-enacting past fashion moments). From the start Issey Miyake worked with traditional Japanese dress structures such as that of the kimono, as well as with folding and layering as in traditional methods of origami; he utilised fabric to create structures and instead of working vertically as many Western designers have done (i.e. beginning at the neck and working down to the hem), his approach views the garment horizontally, asymmetrically and in the round (Figure 7.6).

Establishing her company Comme des Garçons in Tokyo in 1973, the work of Rei Kawakubo was seen as iconoclastic and ground-breaking with its emphasis on black, unusual fabrics and androgynous designs. Her collection

Figure 7.6 Issey Miyake 'Pleats Please' window; part of the World Fashion Window Displays, 27 September 2015, in Tokyo, Japan (photo by Ayumi Kakamu/Getty Images).

was first shown in Paris in 1981. As fashion writer Brenda Pollen observes in an article appositely entitled 'Jagged Edge':

> Both Kawakubo and Yamomoto take an approach to dress that could be described as intellectual and artistic. Neither is happy with the idea of it as a static language … so they both chose to overturn the conventions of dress we take for granted.[37]

For Yamomoto, who studied at the Bunka College of Design, perfection is anathema and so is symmetry, while the space between the body and the fabric is important. He has been described as 'a genius, a philosopher, a man with the vision to overturn our accepted notion of dress entirely'.[38] In a way his approach could be described as 'anti-couture' since it rejected the perfection of the couture garment: both in terms of the perfect fit and the perfectly finished garment.

Deconstruction as applied to fashion is a term which became a catch-all for clothing that challenged conventional body-hugging clothing whose actual construction (seams) is deliberately hidden, as opposed to loose-fitting, often asymmetrical clothing in which the seams might be visible, edges and hems unfinished and left to fray. Although the trend has been attributed first and foremost to Japanese designers among others, designers as diverse as Rei Kawakubo, Yohji Yamomoto, John Richmond and Helen Storey have, observes journalist Debbie Buckett, 'left frayed seams on show, cut uneven hemlines to reveal lining hanging out in crumpled folds and sent their models down the catwalk in collections that are raggedy or recycled'.[39] It was later taken up by

Belgian designers in the 1980s and 1990s. Indeed, deconstruction has been described as 'a bandwagon on to which many have leapt since the heyday of punk'.[40] In an article in the *Independent* in 1993, Richard Martin, curator of the Costume Institute at the Metropolitan Museum of Art in New York, was reported as being keen to acquire pieces of 'deconstructivist' fashion because 'in the future it will indicate the exact point where fashion changed gear'.[41]

Not only did Belgian designers adopt a new and radically different attitude to clothing, they also questioned the traditional ways in which fashion was presented as a dream of a lifestyle available only to the elite and to fashionistas: rejecting the biannual fashion shows, in 1994 Martin Margiela (b. 1957) worked for Jean-Paul Gaultier in Paris before going solo and becoming the 'star' of the Paris collections in 1992 at the age of thirty-five. He presented his collection to press and customers at the time when the clothes actually reached the shops, with shows taking place on the same day in nine stores around the world, modelled by twelve women from each city. He presented them in unusual settings such as subway stations, disused theatres and waiting rooms.[42] The iconoclastic message communicated by Belgian designers has signalled 'the end of traditional images of female beauty, couture and sexuality, and the shreds, tatters and tears of "destroy couture" are seen to reflect the ransacked landscape of the economy'.[43] Margiela himself has been quoted as saying that 'the whole business [of fashion] is in evolution' and that 'fashion as a luxury is redundant and must eventually be replaced by a new reality'.[44] However, the cost of his clothes seems somewhat at odds with his 'philosophy': in the early 1990s the price tags were, for example, around £500 for a skirt put together with old silk scarves and £400 for a short coat reconstructed from jumble-sale jackets. However, Margiela's clothes are beautifully hand-finished with raw edges 'finished' in such a way that they do not fray in the wash while sleeves are shaped with several darts to follow the fluid movement of the arms (Figure 7.7).

Even before the rise to fame of Martin Margiela, British *Elle* featured the now legendary 'Antwerp Six' group of designers in the mid-1980s: Dries Van Noten, Ann Demeulemeester, Dirk Van Saene, Walter Van Beirendonck, Dirk Bikkembergs and Marina Yee. All perfectionists and constantly refining shapes, Dries Van Noten (b. 1958) has, however, been described as the most 'commercial' of the six (Figure 7.8). He was quoted as saying that 'the "total

Figure 7.7 A model walks Martin Margiela's spring 1998 Ready-to-Wear (Prêt-à-Porter) Runway Collection (photo by Guy Marineau/Condé Nast via Getty Images).

look" fashion of the Italians and the Japanese is over' and that 'fashion is about mixing nice shirts, sweaters and jackets in a way that suits your personality, not following the dictates of designers.'[45] By the late 1990s, Ann Demeulemeester (b. 1959) was being described as one of fashion's most emulated designers: 'Her influence has extended into both the collections of other designers and the ever-more-quick-to-react high street.'[46] A graduate of Antwerp's Royal Academy of Fine Art, she first came to public attention in the mid-1980s when she and fellow students who made up the 'Antwerp Six' group hired a truck and headed off to try their luck at London Fashion Week. For Demeulemeester, cut was to become supremely important and her hallmarks at this time were graceful asymmetric T-shirt dresses, softly structured jackets and voluminous, low-slung trousers. Some have described her work as harshly androgynous but Demeulemeester wanted to show that women have both masculine and feminine elements. Her muse became the singer Patti Smith, who wrote poetry to accompany the designer's runway soundtracks (Figure 7.9).

The work of designers from the late twentieth century onwards has contributed to a repositioning of the traditional relationships between the

Figure 7.8 A model walks the runway during Dries Van Noten's show as part of Paris Fashion Week, Womenswear, autumn/winter 2019/2020, on 27 February 2019 (photo by Kristy Sparow/Getty Images Entertainment).

designers and their clients that had developed due to the advent of couture in the late nineteenth century, thus changing the ways in which class in relation to fashion is defined. In the twenty-first century a significant range of new cultural influences has heralded what has been described as the end of fashion as it has evolved over the past two hundred or so years. These will be summarised in the Conclusion.

Figure 7.9 A model walks the runway during the Ann Demeulemeester Menswear autumn/winter 2019/2020 show as part of Paris Fashion Week on 18 January 2019 in Paris, France (photo by Kristy Sparow/Getty Images Entertainment).

Conclusion

At the start of this study, I argued that class and class consciousness grew out of specific historical circumstances and that they continue to be meaningful concepts in twenty-first-century British society. While I have explored some of the changing relationships between fashion and class since the late eighteenth century, finally I want to ask whether fashion is still a reflection of class or, conversely, if class is a prime mover of fashion? Over time, the interdependence of class and fashion that has been the focus of this study has been uncoupled, but arguably that is not because *class* no longer exists, but rather because, and as many have argued recently, *fashion* no longer does. Aside from the privileged, though very small, world of couture and apart from the consumption of luxury, high-end brands, in theory everyone can obtain and wear a version of latest styles and trends. That this is possible is because of the political, technological and cultural changes of the past two hundred or so years, culminating in the high street revolution which democratised fashion in a number of different ways, including those discussed over the course of this study. 'Fashion', argues American fashion writer Teri Agins, 'which began in the hallowed ateliers of Parisian couture, now emanates from designers and retailers from around the world, reaching the masses at every level.'[1] At the end of the twentieth century, Agins argued that 'it's not only the end of the millennium, but the end of fashion as we know it.'[2] In her view, the reasons for the demise of fashion in the United States were as follows: women 'let go of fashion'; people stopped dressing up (e.g. Microsoft Corporation founder Bill Gates, one of the world's wealthiest men, became the 'personification of the Internet-set look, dressed for success in chinos and sports shirts') while overall, people's values changed with regard to fashion:

Stores like Ann Taylor, The Limited, Gap, Banana Republic and J. Crew turned out good-looking clothes that deflated the notion that fashion belonged exclusively to the elite. In effect, designer labels started to seem like a rip-off. Increasingly, it became a badge of honor to be a bargain hunter, even among the well-to-do.[3]

As a further example of this dressing-down culture, in 2016 Robert Armstrong wrote in the *Financial Times* about the 'significance' of the wearing of casual clothing by the privileged, remarking on Boris Johnson's 'devil-may-care style' prior to becoming British foreign secretary, commenting that the latter look is 'usually an expression of privilege'.[4] Celebrities, according to Agins, also play an important role in popularising and influencing trends: since very few people get access to fashion shows the Oscars became very influential with Giorgio Armani being 'forever … remembered as the first designer who swept the Oscars without taking home a single trophy'.[5] In summary, for Agins, the end of fashion was associated with the success of mass marketing:

> But whether fashion promoted jeans or strapless gowns, the rewards would always go to the companies that expertly marketed their way into the collective consciousness of a critical mass of consumers.[6]

The final uncoupling of fashion from class, along with the availability of increasingly cheaper clothing retailed by companies whose priorities are large turnover and 'the bottom line', has occurred because of the advent of the internet. The first two decades of the twenty-first century saw the exponential growth of online shopping for discounted and cheap(er) clothes through websites like ASOS or PrettyLittleThing.com, as well as for designer clothing through companies such as MyTheresa and Net-a-Porter. (ASOS and Net-a-Porter both opened their virtual doors in 2000.) Online shopping, we are told, is largely responsible for the downturn of the high street. Furthermore, the accessibility of designer websites where anyone with access to the internet can watch the catwalk shows featuring the latest collections has democratised fashion in another way: before the internet the couture and ready-to-wear shows were the exclusive domains of a small group of clients and fashion press. That is no longer the case.

The transformation of more casual clothing into 'fashion' along with the purchase of such clothing online (purchasing before you try on) has eroded the significance of good fit as a major contributor to making a decision about buying an item of clothing; ironic then that, as we have seen (Chapter 5), issues around sizing constituted a major hurdle in the historical development of the ready-to-wear clothing industry. The advent of sportswear has resulted in trainers, hoodies and joggers becoming the fall-back everyday look, where comfort and 'cool' reign supreme while fit and individuality are fast-disappearing priorities. The relative unimportance of good fit has enabled further growth of this industry, rather than holding it back as it did in the nineteenth century. On a manufacturing level it is so much simpler to make a range of garments in, say, 'XS-S', 'M-L' and so on than it is to grade a whole range of sizes from 4 to 22. Powerful brands selling sportswear such as Adidas and Nike have made a major, recent contribution to the disassociation between fashion and class. In this case, fashion – if this *is* fashion – no longer distinguishes class and class no longer determines fashion. The growth of social media meanwhile means not only that individuals who otherwise have no particular role within the fashion industry can be extraordinarily powerful 'influencers', but that teenagers have, arguably, become more interested in constructing an identity online than making an outward show of their allegiances and interests. This is democratisation arrived at its logical conclusion: fashion was defined in large part by its relationship to class but once that relationship has been severed, this is arguably the end of fashion as we have known it for at least the past two centuries.

But there is another movement that is now fully underway: the backlash against fast fashion and the quest for a change of people's buying and consumer habits (Figure C.1). The term 'fast fashion' was first coined by the *New York Times* in 1989 to describe Zara's 'Quick Response' model.[7] A good example of the 'success' of the fast-fashion model was seen during the launch of Primark UK stores in 2007, when shoppers were seen trampling each other to get in.[8] Andrew Brooks observes that fast fashion not only encapsulates the rapid changes in trends and styles found in the 'Global North' and the pace of retail sales, but also the speed at which designs can be transmitted around the world and orders turned into garments.[9] Since the beginning of the twenty-first century and partly in response to increasing awareness of, and research into, climate change – former US vice-president Al Gore's hard-hitting 2006 documentary 'An Inconvenient Truth' is about the reality and implications

Figure C.1 A Greenpeace activist stands with her banner in the window of Zara in Budapest (20 November 2012) during a demonstration against street fashion brands (photo by Attila Kisbenedek/AFP/Getty Images).

of global warming – the fashion industry has been forced to take and give account of its demands on depleting world resources. Those 'demands' are considered both in terms of the raw materials themselves, including 'natural' cotton and fabrics such as viscose (the latter a contributor to the depletion of the world's forests), but also in terms of the vast quantities of water used in the manufacture of fabrics such as denim, and quite apart from the chemical pollution caused by manufacturing and finishing processes – including dyeing – of both natural and man-made fabrics. Even those more expensive brands such as White Company and Phase Eight valued initially by customers for selling natural fabrics such as silk seem to have mostly sold out to polyester as an alternative to silk. The fabric may feel soft and drape well but few are probably aware of polyester's polluting 'qualities'.

This is Greenpeace on 'synthetic fibers':

> Synthetic fibers could be a wonderful thing. Their production requires far less water than cotton and they don't require toxic pesticides to grow. But does that make them environmentally friendly? Sadly not.

The expansion of fast fashion wouldn't be possible without polyester. Relatively cheap and easily available, polyester is now used in about 60% of our clothes. But, if we take into account the fossil fuels used in its production, CO2 emissions for polyester clothing are nearly three times higher than for cotton! Our reliance on polyester is one of the reasons why the fashion industry is one of the most polluting industries in the world; both in terms of its emissions-heavy production and the non-biodegradable waste it leaves behind.

One piece of clothing can release 700,000 fibers in a single wash. Once our clothes reach a washing machine, the synthetic fabrics release tiny strands: so-called microfibers. These are essentially microscopic pieces of plastic, just like the microbeads you find in cosmetics. Every time you run your washing machine, hundreds of thousands of microfibers are flushed down the drain. Many reach beaches and oceans where they can remain for hundreds of years. Swallowed by fish and other sealife, microplastic travels up the food chain, where they end up on our plates.[10]

The world's population is increasing: globally it has increased from 1 billion in 1800 to 7.6 billion in 2017, and the United Nations has predicted that it will reach 8.6 billion by 2030 and 9.8 billion by 2050.[11] As Greenpeace has pointed out, the average Western customer now buys 60 per cent more clothes a year and keeps them for about half as long as fifteen years ago.[12] The paradox is this: on the one hand, there is the focus on growth that is at the heart of capitalist business models and which is key to companies finding ever cheaper ways to produce clothing for increasing populations who, we are told, 'want' more and more 'disposable' and cheaper clothing; and on the other hand, there is the urgent need to address how we make, consume and care for our clothes to mitigate what has become the cultural 'necessity' of consumption.

What has been the response in the fashion literature since then? There has been a torrent of publications devoted to 'eco-chic' such as Matilda Lee's *Eco-Chic: The Savvy Shopper's Guide to Ethical Fashion* which tells readers that 'with this book as your guide you can look great and change the world at the same time.'[13] The book comes with a directory of ethical fashion companies and a 'dictionary' of definitions. Sandy Black's *Eco-Chic: The Fashion Paradox* (2011) is accompanied by suggestions for further reading and a glossary of organisations related to sustainable fashion. The entire issue of the magazine

Marie-Claire was devoted to ethical fashion in June 2008: 'eco-chic goes glam', the cover page announces. Marie O'Riordan's editor's letter proclaimed that 'if we can save the planet while maintaining our place in the style stakes, all is surely good'.[14] It is clearly more complex than this.

On the high street Marks & Spencer seemed to lead the way with their Plan A:

> Plan A is Marks & Spencer's eco and ethical programme that tackles both today's and tomorrow's sustainable retail challenges. Plan A was launched in 2007 and given its name because we think there is no Plan B for our one planet. We're committed to helping to build a sustainable future by being a business that enables our customers to have a positive impact on wellbeing, communities and the planet through all we do.[15]

In 2018, the company published a fifty-one-page report on the progress made since the launch of Plan A 2025 in 2017. While M&S's actions are to be applauded – for example, manufacturing fleeces from recycled plastic bottles and introducing ranges of organic cotton T-shirts – as long as businesses are focused on expansion rather than consolidation these moves might be described by some as tokenism. It is perhaps telling that the flagship 'eco' store in Bournemouth (Dorset) town centre closed down in 2018. The real barrier to finding a solution to the Western addiction to fast fashion from within the fashion industry is that these industries are mostly built on expansionist business models that are in direct opposition to 'slow' fashion. And, more generally, while it is imperative that we do away with plastic bags, plastic packaging and plastic coffee cups, why, one might ask, did supermarkets introduce them and create the 'demand' in the first place? Likewise, why encourage the consumption models that characterise 'fast fashion'? Retailers may argue that the customer demands 'choice', but there doesn't seem to be a lot of variety among the endless rails of cheap, 'Made in China' polyester clothing in the mass fashion sector.

A more reflective approach based on research has come from the education sector. Part of the challenge has been to highlight the global problems that excessive consumption and fast fashion have brought with them. Kate Fletcher describes the situation thus:

> Fashion is readily characterized as the poster-industry of consumerist materialism; as frivolous, superficial and evanescent; a sector that delivers

change without development. It is shaped by the superfluity of mass production and unlimited consumption; an industry linked to abysmal abuses of workers' rights, resource intensive and polluting supply chains, waste generation, ideas predicated on the image, on status competition and ownership, on individualised success.[16]

The work done by the Centre for Sustainable Fashion (London College of Fashion, University of the Arts) since its establishment in 2008 is pioneering in this respect. In November 2018 the Centre hosted a remarkable two-day conference in partnership with the Global Fashion Conference entitled 'What's Going On? A Discourse on Fashion, Design and Sustainability'. It brought together people from education and industry (both global brands as well as independent companies) to focus on pioneering sustainable approaches to fashion in a series of lectures, workshops and lively debate. Furthermore, a knowledge of history provides insights into the ways in which in the past clothes were repaired, relined, retrimmed and altered to extend their use, cut down for children's garments, handed to relatives and dependants, and passed on as perks to servants to use as they wished and many of these clothes were sold on to the second-hand market.[17]

In the contemporary context, questions are being asked about how we should educate young designers and those wishing to enter the fashion industry. The challenge is evident if, as Helen Storey advised, 'designers should be looking at why they want to be designers in a world that doesn't need them'.[18] It has been pointed out that we, as customers, should be more demanding by asking where the raw materials and fabrics we wear come from and who made the clothing we are buying. Andrew Brooks shows how difficult this question is to answer as it is well-nigh impossible to audit, say, a pair of jeans, given that, depending on whether one is talking about where the fabric is sourced or made, printed or dyed or where the garment is stitched, finished and packaged, these processes can take place in a large number of locations.[19] And even more challenging is to ask consumers to think twice about whether they actually need a new item of clothing, just as the company Patagonia did in a brave advertisement in the *New York Times* on Black Friday on 25 November 2011 admonishing (potential) customers, 'Don't buy this jacket'.

In 2014 Lidewij Edelkoort of Trend Union, the respected and highly influential fashion forecaster, published her 'Manifesto for the Next Decade'.

It was, significantly, entitled *Anti-Fashion* and in it she summarised her 'ten reasons [for] why the fashion system is obsolete'.[20] Deploring the way in which the world of fashion marketing had taken over from fashion and along with it, consumer choice, Edelkoort predicts how 'the consumers of today and tomorrow are going to choose for themselves, creating and designing their own wardrobes'.[21] She goes on to say that 'they will share clothes amongst each other since ownership doesn't mean a thing anymore. They will rent clothes, lend clothes, transform clothes and find clothes on the streets'.[22] While the lone designer may have become obsolete with people working in teams increasingly important, on the other hand she predicts that couture will make a comeback, occupying the void left by fashion:

> After all it is in the atelier of couture that we will find the laboratory of this labor of love. Suddenly the profession of couturier will become coveted and the exclusive way of crafting couture will be inspiring all others.[23]

It is impossible to predict the next few decades but if Edelkoort is correct, then could the revival of couture reverse some of the trends of the past century, or is classless 'fashion' here to stay? In any case, the enormous and urgent challenge for the future of those industries that make and sell clothing – and of course for us as customers and consumers who have the power to make the choices of what to buy and what not to buy – is both to change our approach to what Brooks calls 'commodity fetishism' ('ethically produced goods', he asserts, 'are an attempt to defetichize the commodity')[24] and to demand sustainable manufacturing processes alongside what Kate Fletcher calls the 'craft of use' ('a glimpse of fashion provision and expression beyond consumerism') applied to the clothing that we already have.[25] Trends that have already become significant since the beginning of the twenty-first century – repurposing, reusing and recycling including buying second-hand and 'vintage' – are a positive contribution. But for these practices to make a significant difference they need to move from being demanded by a relatively small group of people to occupying mainstream culture: in short, they need to be democratised.

Notes

Introduction

1 Richard Allestree, *The Whole Duty of Man* (London, 1671), 194.

2 Alexandra Warwick and Dani Cavallaro, *Fashioning the Frame: Boundaries, Dress and the Body* (Oxford: Berg, 1998), xvii.

3 Linda O'Keefe, *Shoes: A Celebration of Pumps, Sandals, Slippers and More* (New York: Workman Publishing, 1996), 348.

4 Ibid., 79.

5 Ibid., 132–5.

6 Frank McCourt, *Angela's Ashes: A Memoir of a Childhood* (London: HarperCollins, 1996).

7 The Shoe Museum in Marikina, Metro Manila, Philippines, houses eight hundred pairs of her shoes.

8 Edwina Ehrman (ed.), *Fashioned from Nature* (London: V&A Publishing, 2018), 21 and 27.

9 Susan Vincent, *Dressing the Elite: Clothes in Early Modern England* (Oxford: Berg, 2003), 4.

10 E. P. Thompson, *The Making of the English Working Class* (London: Virago, 2012).

11 Marilynne Robinson, *When I Was a Child I Read Books* (London: Virago, 2012), 86.

12 Board of Trade, 'Patriotic Patches' (London, 1943), 1. Quoted in Selina Todd, *The Rise and Fall of the Working Class 1910–2010* (London: John Murray, 2014), 140.

13 Valerie Mendes, *Black in Fashion* (London: V&A Publications, 1999), 100–101.

14 Vincent, *Dressing the Elite*, 6.

15 Robert Colls, 'The Making and the Man', *Times Higher Education Supplement* (21 November 2013): 45.

1 What's in a name? The language of class in relation to fashion and fabrics

1 Diana Crane, *Fashion and Its Social Agendas: Class, Gender, and Identity in Clothing* (Chicago: University of Chicago Press, 2000), 3.

2 Selina Todd, *The Rise and Fall of the Working Class, 1910–2010* (London: John Murray, 2014), 1.

3 Robert Colls, 'The Making and the Man', *Times Higher Education Supplement* (21 November 2013): 45.

4 Todd, *The Rise and Fall of the Working Class*, 108.

5 Ibid., 101.

6 Ibid., 143.

7 Suzanne Moore, 'The Left Doesn't Understand Working-Class Tories', *Guardian* (14 May 2015): 5.

8 Todd, *The Rise and Fall of the Working Class*, 338.

9 Danny Dorling, 'Just Who Do You Think You Are?', *Times Higher Education Supplement* (12 November 2015): 50. This is a review of *Social Class in the 21st Century*, edited by Mike Savage (London: Pelican, 2015).

10 Patrick Joyce, *Visions of the People: Industrial England and the Question of Class, 1840–1914* (Cambridge: Cambridge University Press, 1991), 21.

11 Crane, *Fashion and Its Social Agendas*, 4.

12 Todd, *The Rise and Fall of the Working Class*, 1.

13 Ibid., 14.

14 Vivienne Richmond (ed.), *Clothing, Society and Culture in Nineteenth-Century England*, vol. 3: *Working-Class Dress* (London: Pickering & Chatto, 2013), xi.

15 D. H. Lawrence, *The Rainbow* (1915; this edn, Harmondsworth: Penguin, 1981), ch. VIII, 270.

16 Virginia Woolf, *A Room of One's Own* (1928; this edn, London: Penguin, 2004), 103.

17 E. P. Thompson, *The Making of the English Working Class* (London: Pelican, 1963), preface, 1.

18 Peter Laslett, *The World We Have Lost* (1965; this edn, Cambridge: Cambridge University Press, 1979), 23–4.

19 Elizabeth Bullen, 'Class', in *Keywords for English Literature*, edited by Philip Nel and Lissa Paul (New York: New York University Press, 2011), 48. Bullen also provides some useful background:

> The word 'class' comes to English from the Latin *classis* via the French *classe*. It first appears in Thomas Blount's *Glossographia* (1656), where he defined it in the language of the times as 'an order or distribution of people according to their several Degrees'. Citing Blount, the *Oxford English Dictionary* traces the term's origins to its use by Servius Tullius who, seeking to raise funds for the Roman military, conducted a census for the purpose of taxing citizens according to their means. He created six categories or classes, based on property or net wealth. In spite of the strong resonance of its etymology with contemporary socioeconomic understandings of class, when it first entered the English language *classe* had greater purchase in reference to a division of scholars or students, and later as a natural history term. (48)

20 Laslett, *The World We Have Lost*, 47.

21 Susan Vincent, *Dressing the Elite: Clothes in Early Modern England* (Oxford: Berg, 2003), 6.

22 Todd, *The Rise and Fall of the Working Class*, 366.

23 Neil McKendrick, John Brewer and J. H. Plumb, *The Birth of a Consumer Society: The Commercialisation of Eighteenth-Century England* (London: Europa Publications, 1982), 53.

24 Patrick Joyce, *Class* (Oxford: Oxford University Press, 1995), 3.

25 Ben Fine and Ellen Leopold, *The World of Consumption* (London: Routledge, 1993), 93.

26 This book was updated in 2010 by PYMCA (Photographic Youth Music Culture Archive).

27 Patrick Joyce, *Visions of the People: Industrial England and the Question of Class 1840–1914* (Cambridge: Cambridge University Press, 1991), 1.

28 Ibid., 10.

29 Ibid., 5. The term 'people' is adopted in two – otherwise very different – studies of non-elite dress: John Styles, *The Dress of the People: Everyday Fashion in Eighteenth-Century England* (New Haven: Yale University Press, 2007); and Rachel Worth, *Fashion for the People: A History of Clothing at Marks & Spencer* (Oxford: Berg 2007).

30 Joyce, *Class*, 11.

31 Patrick Curry, 'Towards a Post-Marxist Social History: Thompson, Clark and Beyond', in *Rethinking Social History: English Society 1570–1920 and Its Interpretation*, edited by Adrian Wilson (Manchester: Manchester University Press, 1993), 179. See also Craig Calhoun, *The Question of Class Struggle: Social Foundations of Popular Radicalism during the Industrial Revolution* (Oxford: Basil Blackwell, 1982).

32 R. S. Neale, *Class and Ideology in the Nineteenth Century* (London: Routledge and Kegan Paul, 1972), 30.

33 Howard Newby, *Country Life: A Social History of Rural England* (London: Weidenfeld and Nicolson, 1987), 54.

34 Alun Howkins, 'Labour History and the Rural Poor 1850–1980', *Rural History* 1:1 (1990): 118.

35 G. E. Mingay, *Rural Life in Victorian England* (Stroud: Alan Sutton Publishing, 1990), 105.

36 Newby, *Country Life*, 13.

37 E. J. Hobsbawm and George Rudé, *Captain Swing* (1969; this edn, Harmondsworth: Penguin, 1985), 4.

38 Howkins, 'Labour History and the Rural Poor 1850–1900', 118 and 117.

39 Ian Dyck, 'Towards the "Cottage Charter": The Expressive Culture of Farm Workers in Nineteenth-Century England', *Rural History* 1:1 (1990): 106 and 107.

40 Colls, 'The Making and the Man', 45.

41 Joyce, *Class*, 10.

42 William Cobbett, *Rural Rides* (1830; this edn with an introduction by George Woodcock, Harmondsworth: Penguin, 1987), 180.

43 Parliamentary Papers, *Second Report from the Commissioners on the Employment of Children, Young Persons and Women in Agriculture, with Appendix Part I and Part II*, 1868–9 (Shannon: Irish University Press, 1968): see, for example, appendix part II, 72.

44 Alexander Somerville, *The Whistler at the Plough – Containing Travels, Statistics and Descriptions of Scenery and Agricultural Customs in Most Parts of England* (1852; this edn with an introduction by Keith D. M. Snell, London: Merlin Press, 1979), 416.

45 Richard Jefferies, 'Wiltshire Labourers', *The Times* (12 November 1872); published here in *Landscape with Figures: An Anthology of Richard Jefferies' Prose* (Harmondsworth: Penguin, 1983), 30.

46 Paul A. Pickering, 'Class without Words: Symbolic Communication in the Chartist Movement', *Past and Present* 112 (1986): 162. Pickering concludes: 'Herein lay the central significance of fustian – it was an unmistakable emblem of "class". Into the cloth was woven the shared experiences and identity of working-class life' (160).

47 Joseph Arch, *Joseph Arch: The Story of His Life Told by Himself* (1898; this edn, London: MacGibbon & Kee, 1966).

48 Peter Davidson, *The Last of the Light: About Twilight* (London: Reaktion, 2015), 99.

49 Todd, *The Rise and Fall of the Working Class*, 53.

50 Ibid., 52.

51 Jennifer Craik, *The Face of Fashion: Cultural Studies in Fashion* (London: Routledge, 1993), 3.

52 Theodore Veblen, *The Theory of the Leisure Class: An Economic Study in the Evolution of Institutions* (New York: Macmillan, 1899).

53 Georg Simmel, 'Fashion', *International Quarterly* 10:1 (October 1904): 138–9.

54 Todd, *The Rise and Fall of the Working Class*, 44.

55 Maria Tamboukou, *Sewing, Writing and Fighting: Radical Practices in Work, Politics and Culture* (London: Rowman and Littlefield, 2016), 63.

56 Pierre Bourdieu, *Distinction: A Social Critique of the Judgment of Taste* (first published in France in 1979; this edn trans. Richard Nice, London: Routledge and Kegan Paul, 1984).

57 Crane, *Fashion and Its Social Agendas*, 7.

58 Bourdieu, *Distinction*, 1–2.

59 Crane, *Fashion and Its Social Agendas*, 8.

60 Ibid., 26.

61 Bourdieu, *Distinction*, 200–201.

62 Ibid., 13.

2 The politics of fashion

1 Ferdinand Braudel, *Civilisation and Capitalism 15th to 18th Century*, 3 vols (London, 1981), vol. I, *The Structures of Everyday Life*, 323.

2 Charles Dickens, *A Tale of Two Cities* (1859; this edition, Harmondsworth: Penguin, 1980), Book the Second, ch. 24.

3 Ibid., Book the Third, ch. 1.

4 Ibid., ch. 9.

5 Ibid., Book the Second, ch. 8.

6 Ibid., ch. 23. The reference to the red cap is to the French 'bonnet rouge' and the reference to wooden shoes is to French 'sabots' or clogs which were associated with French working-class dress, discussed in more detail later.

7 Ibid., ch. 6.

8 Ibid., Book the Third, ch. 2.

9 Ibid., ch. 13.

10 Ibid., Book the Second, ch. 18.

11 Ibid., Book the Third, ch. 16.

12 Ibid., Book the Second, ch. 15.

13 Ibid.

14 Susan Vincent, *Dressing the Elite: Clothes in Early Modern England* (Oxford: Berg, 2003), 118.

15 Linda Welters and Abby Lillethun (eds), *The Fashion Reader* (Oxford: Berg, 2007), 4.

16 Vincent, *Dressing the Elite*, 120 and 122.

17 Richard Allestree, *The Whole Duty of Man* (London, 1671), 210.

18 Vincent, *Dressing the Elite*, 62–3.

19 Ibid., 9.

20 Rebecca Arnold, *Fashion: A Very Short Introduction* (Oxford: Oxford University Press, 2009), 98.

21 Kimberley Chrisman-Campbell, 'From Baroque Elegance to the French Revolution 1700–1790', in *The Fashion Reader*, edited by Linda Welters and Abby Lillethun (Oxford: Berg, 2007), 6.

22 See Elizabeth Ewing, *Fur in Dress* (London: B.T. Batsford, 1981).

23 Marjorie Wiseman, 'Acquisition or Inheritance? Material Goods in Paintings by Vermeer and His Contemporaries', in *Vermeer and the Masters of Genre*

Painting: Inspiration and Rivalry, edited by Adrian E. Waiboer (New Haven: Yale University Press, 2017), 59.

24 In a different context, Marcia Pointon discusses the meanings of clothes and buttons, for example, in portraits of men. She argues that irrespective of whether they existed or not, or whether they are direct imitations of something that had a presence in the real world, 'they construct in a peculiarly assertive and seductive way, a rhetorical narrative of socialized elite masculinity'. See Marcia Pointon, *Portrayal and the Search for Identity* (London: Reaktion, 2013), 125.

25 Daniel Roche, *The Culture of Clothing: Dress and Fashion in the Ancien Régime* (first published in 1989 and translated into English in 1994; this edn, Cambridge: Cambridge University Press, 1996), see especially 151–83.

26 Vincent, *Dressing the Elite*, 33.

27 Jean-Jacques Rousseau, *Reveries of the Solitary Walker* (first published anonymously in 1792; this translation with an introduction by Peter France (Harmondsworth: Penguin, 1979), Fifth Walk, 84; Third Walk, 51.

28 Roche, *The Culture of Clothing*, 33.

29 Ibid., 149.

30 Jean-Jacques Rousseau, 'Considération sur les avantages de changer le costume français par la société populaire et républicaine des Arts', *La Décade philosophique littéraire et politique*, 10 Floréal, Year III: 60–2. Quoted in ibid., 151.

31 Pointon, *Portrayal and the Search for Identity*, 122.

32 Christopher Breward, *The Culture of Fashion* (Manchester: Manchester University Press, 1995), 114.

33 Chrisman-Campbell, 'From Baroque Elegance to the French Revolution 1700–1790', 14.

34 Le Brun, *Le Journal de la Mode et du Goût*, 13me cahier, 25 June 1791.

35 Le Brun, *Le Journal de la Mode et du Goût*, 11me cahier, 5 June 1790.

36 Chrisman-Campbell, 'From Baroque Elegance to the French Revolution 1700–1790', 17.

37 Le Brun, *Le Journal de la Mode et du Goût*, 10me cahier, 1 June 1792.

38 Aileen Ribeiro, *Fashion in the French Revolution* (London: Batsford, 1988), 46.

39 Le Brun, *Le Journal de la Mode et du Goût*, 1er cahier, 25 February 1790.

40 Le Brun, *Le Journal de la Mode et du Goût*, 19me cahier, 25 August 1790.

41 Le Brun, *Le Journal de la Mode et du Goût*, 27me cahier, 20 November 1792.

42 Roche, *The Culture of Clothing*, 146.

43 Valerie Steele, 'The Social and Political Significance of Macaroni Fashion', *Costume* 19 (1985): 94–109.

44 Roche, *The Culture of Clothing*, 139.

45 Le Brun, *Le Journal de la Mode et du Goût*, 23me cahier, 5 October 1790.

46 Le Brun, *Le Journal de la Mode et du Goût*, 9me cahier 15 May 1790 and 36me cahier, 15 February 1791, respectively.

47 Ribeiro, *Fashion in the French Revolution*, 141.

48 Le Brun, *Le Journal de la Mode et du Goût*, 22me cahier, 25 September 1790: 'Il y a plus de dix ans que le taffetas n'avoit été autant à la mode qu'il l'est aujourdh'hui.' He goes on to say that although linen has lost a little of its vogue, it will always be 'le fond' of women's undergarments. For reference to unpowdered hair, see 5me cahier, 5 April 1791.

49 Roche, *The Culture of Clothing*, 314.

50 Ibid., 326–7.

51 Ibid., 327.

52 Honoré de Balzac, *Old Goriot* (1835; this edn translated with an introduction by A. J. Krailsheimer, Oxford World's Classics: Oxford University Press, 2009), ch. 2, 105.

3 Fabric of society: technological change and fashion

1 Andrew Brooks, *Clothing Poverty: The Hidden World of Fast Fashion and Second Hand Clothes* (London: Zed Books, 2015), 55 and 62.

2 Giorgio Riello, *Cotton: The Fabric That Made the Modern World* (Cambridge: Cambridge University Press, 2013), xxiv.

3 Ibid., 12.

4 Beverly Lemire, *Fashion's Favourite: The Cotton Trade and the Consumer in Britain, 1660–1800* (Oxford: Pasold Research Fund/Oxford University Press, 1991).

5 Riello, *Cotton*, 39–40.

6 Ibid., 49.

7 Ibid., 52.

8 Ibid., 80.

9 Ibid., 74–5.

10 Ibid., 86. Riello later 'renames' this triangular trade (describing it as a 'diamond' trade) to include India because of the latter's long history of exporting cottons (ibid., 139).

11 Ibid., 100.

12 Daniel Roche, *The Culture of Clothing: Dress and Fashion in the Ancien Régime* (first published in 1989 and translated into English in 1994; this edn, Cambridge: Cambridge University Press, 1996), 138.

13 Riello, *Cotton*, 115–16.

14 Ibid., 96–7.

15 Ibid., 98–9.

16 Ibid., 119.

17 Ibid., 123.

18 Ibid., 130–1.

19 Kimberley Chrisman-Campbell, 'From Baroque Elegance to the French. Revolution 1700–1790', in *The Fashion Reader*, edited by Linda Welters and Abby Lillethun (Oxford: Berg, 2007), 18.

20 Riello, *Cotton*, 149.

21 Ibid., 211–12. In the 1770s, woollens contributed to the overall textile production of Britain 60 per cent of net value-added; by 1821 this figure had fallen to 34 per cent. In the same period, the contribution of textiles overall to GDP increased from 9 per cent to 14 per cent (252). These figures reveal the declining importance of woollens relative to cotton textiles.

22 Ibid., 254. There was, however, disruption to these supplies during the American Civil War (1861–5).

23 Fanny Burney, *Evelina* (1778; this edition, Oxford: Oxford University Press, 1987), vol. 1, letter X, 27.

24 Ibid.

25 Penelope Byrde, *Jane Austen Fashion: Fashion and Needlework in the Works of Jane Austen* (Ludlow: Excellent Press, 1999), 32.

26 Burney, *Evelina*, vol. 1, letter X, 27–8; emphasis in the original.

27 Ibid., 28.

28 Ibid., vol. 1, letter XVI, 59.

29 Ibid., 61.

30 Byrde, *Jane Austen Fashion*, 13.

31 Jane Austen, *Sense and Sensibility* (1811; this edn, London: Penguin Classic Random House, 2014), vol. 2, ch. xiv (but numbered as ch. 36 in this revised version), 234; emphasis in the original.

32 Burney, *Evelina*, vol. I, letter XVII, 69.

33 Ibid., vol. II, letter XVI, 212.

34 Ibid., 207.

35 Ibid., vol. I, letter XXI, 84–92.

36 Ibid., vol. I, letter XX, 79–80; emphases in the original.

37 Ibid., vol. I, letter XVI, 65 and vol. I, letter XVII, 67.

38 Ibid., vol. II, letter II, 148; emphases in the original.

39 Ibid., 149.

40 Byrde, *Jane Austen Fashion*, 65.

41 Ibid., 66.

42 Burney, *Evelina*, vol. II, letter XIX, 219; emphasis in the original.

43 Ibid., 222; emphasis in the original.

44 Lemire, *Fashion's Favourite*, 164.

45 Ibid., 99.

46 John Styles, *Threads of Feeling: The London Foundling Hospital's Textile Tokens, 1740–1770* (London: The Foundling Museum, 2010), 34.

47 Ibid., 39.

48 Lemire, *Fashion's Favourite*, 190.

4 From north to south: class identity and dress in the English novel, 1820–60

1 George Eliot, *The Mill on the Floss* (1860; this edn, Edinburgh: William and Blackwood and Sons, 1860), Book Sixth, ch. V, 366.

2 J. A. V. Chapple and A. Pollard, *The Letters of Mrs* Gaskell (Manchester: Manchester University Press, 1966), letter to Marianne Gaskell, 24 April 1865, no. 566 (752). The analysis of the role of dress in Elizabeth Gaskell's novels in this chapter is discussed in Rachel Worth, 'Elizabeth Gaskell, Clothes and Class Identity', *Costume* 32 (1998): 52–9.

3 Elizabeth Gaskell, *Mary Barton* (first published anonymously in 1848 in two volumes by Chapman and Hall; this edn, Harmondsworth: Penguin Classics, 1970; with an introduction by Stephen Gill), preface, 37.

4 Elizabeth Gaskell, *North and South* (first published in Dickens's *Household Words* in twenty-two weekly instalments, September 1854 to January 1855. It was first published in novel form in 1855. Here, references are made to the Penguin Popular Classics edn, 1994), ch. V, 50.

5 Jane Tozer and Sarah Levitt, *Fabric of Society: A Century of People and Their Clothes, 1770–1870* (Carno: Laura Ashley, 1983), 37.

6 Ibid.

7 Gaskell, *Mary Barton*, ch. 1, 45.

8 Selina Todd, *The Rise and Fall of the Working Class, 1910–2010* (London: John Murray, 2014), 1.

9 Gaskell, *Mary Barton*, ch. 8, 130.

10 Ibid., ch. 16, 233.

11 See *Encyclopedia of Textiles* edited by the American Fabrics Magazine (Doric Publishing Co., 1960): 'Fustian was a low quality, coarse cotton cloth first made in the Fustat or Ghetto area outside the city of Cairo. The Egyptians used a double cloth construction, which, despite the fact that it was regarded as an inferior material, gave long wear. Some better-grade cloths were made from linen.' Fustian later changed from the original material, implying, as a generic term,

'heavy cotton goods in the order of beaverteen, corduroy, doeskin, moleskin, and velveteen' (252). The 'fustians' worn in England in the eighteenth century and referred to in Chapter 3 were a mixture of linen and cotton.

12 Friedrich Engels, *The Condition of the Working Class in England in 1844* (first authorised English translation was published in New York in 1887 and in London in 1892. This edn, Granada Publishing, 1969; with an introduction by Eric Hobsbawm), 99.

13 George Eliot, *Felix Holt, the Radical* (Edinburgh: William Blackwood and Sons, 1866), ch. XI, 121.

14 Ibid., ch. XXIX, 253.

15 Engels, *The Condition of the Working Class in England in 1844*, 99.

16 Gaskell, *North and South*, ch. XXXI, 302.

17 Ibid., ch. XXVIII, 267.

18 Ibid., ch. XXXIII, 319.

19 Gaskell, *Mary Barton*, ch. 15, 227.

20 Ibid., 128.

21 Jenny Uglow, *A Habit of Stories* (London: Faber and Faber, 1993), 370.

22 Gaskell, *North and South*, ch. XIII, 116.

23 Ibid., ch. VIII, 81.

24 Charles Kingsley, *Yeast* (published in Fraser's Magazine in 1848 and in book form in 1851; this edn, London: Macmillan, 1895), ch. XIV, 199.

25 Ibid., ch. VI, 85.

26 Ibid., ch. VIII, 98.

27 Ibid., ch. XIII, 177. Earlier in the chapter Tregarva comments that free schools, penny clubs, clothing clubs 'all make the matter worse' (174).

28 This topic is discussed in more detail in Rachel Worth, *Clothing and Landscape in Victorian England: Working-Class Dress and Rural Life* (London: I. B. Tauris, 2018), especially ch. 2.

29 Kingsley, *Yeast*, ch. IX, 117.

30 Ibid., ch. XI, 155.

31 Parliamentary Papers, *Second Report from the Commissioners on the Employment of Children, Young Persons and Women in Agriculture (1868–9)*, Appendix Part I, 152.

32 Ibid., 141.

33 Marghanita Laski, *George Eliot and Her World* (London: Thames and Hudson, 1978), 55.

34 Ibid., 18.

35 George Eliot, *Adam Bede* (first published in serial form in Blackwood's Magazine, the first part appearing in the February edition of 1859; this edn, Harmondsworth: Penguin Popular Classics, 1994), ch. XXXVI, 355.

36 Ibid., ch. 1, 24.

37 Ibid., ch. IV, 60.

38 Ibid., 50.

39 Ibid., ch. VI, 81.

40 Ibid., ch. XVIII, 199.

41 Ibid., 183.

42 Ibid., 184.

43 Ibid., ch. XX, 219.

44 Ibid., ch. II, 33.

45 Ibid., 31.

46 Ibid., 41.

47 Ibid., ch. VII, 90.

48 Ibid., ch. V, 69.

49 Ibid., ch. IX, 104–5.

50 Ibid., ch. XV, 151.

51 Ibid., ch. XXII, 244.

52 Ibid., ch. XII, 133.

53 Ibid., ch. XXV, 267.

54 Eliot, *Felix Holt, the Radical*, ch. XXXIX, 335.

55 Ibid., ch. V, 64.

56 Anthony Trollope, *The Warden* (1855; this edn, London: J.M. Dent and Sons Ltd, 1907), ch. V, 72.

57 Ibid., ch. II, 20.

58 Ibid., ch. I, 9.

59 Wilkie Collins, *No Name* (published in serial form 1862–63, three-volume edition published in December 1862 by Sampson Low, Son and Co.; this edn, Oxford: Oxford University Press, 1986), 186.

60 Ibid., Second Scene, ch. I, 194.

61 Ibid., ch. III, 233.

62 Ibid., Between the Scenes, ch. IX, 254.

63 Ibid., Third Scene, ch. I, 262 and she again describes herself as such in Third Scene, ch. IV, 304.

64 Ibid., Fourth Scene, ch. II, 350.

65 Ibid., ch. VII, 405–6.

66 Ibid., ch. II, 355.

67 Ibid., Sixth Scene, ch. II, 613.

68 Ibid., Seventh Scene, ch. I, 621.

69 Trollope, *The Warden*, ch. VI, 87.

70 Peter Keating, *The Haunted Study: A Social History of the English Novel, 1875–1914* (London: Fontana Press, 1991), see especially 186 and 285.

5 Fashion, class and democratisation

1 William Cobbett, *Rural Rides* (1830; this edn, Harmondsworth: Penguin, 1987), 475.

2 Aldous Huxley, *Brave New World* (1932; this edn, London: Flamingo, 1994), 49.

3 Sarah Levitt, *Fashion in Photographs, 1880–1900* (London: Batsford, 1991), 13.

4 Diana Crane, *Fashion and Its Social Agendas: Class, Gender and Identity in Clothing* (Chicago: University of Chicago Press, 2000), 62.

5 Thomas Hardy, 'The Dorsetshire Labourer', *Longman's Magazine*, vol. 2 (1883): 252–69, especially 262–3.

6 Crane, *Fashion and Its Social Agendas*, 26.

7 Diary entry for 14 February 1890, cited in Carole Seymour-Jones, *Woman of Conflict* (London: Allison and Busby, 1992), 184.

8 Jennifer Craik, *The Face of Fashion: Cultural Studies in Fashion* (London: Routledge, 1993), 47.

9 H. Llewellyn Smith (ed.), *The New Survey of London Life and Labour*, vol. 2 (London: King & Son, 1930), 192–3. Quoted in Christopher Breward, *Fashioning London: Clothing and the Modern Metropolis* (Oxford: Berg, 2004), 102.

10 Christopher Breward, Edwina Ehrman and Caroline Evans, *The London Look: Fashion from Street to Catwalk* (New Haven: Yale University Press and the Museum of London, 2004); Frank Mort, *Cultures of Consumption, Masculinities and Social Space in Late Twentieth-Century Britain* (London: Routledge, 1996).

11 Ben Fine and Ellen Leopold, *The World of Consumption* (London: Routledge, 1993), 93.

12 Neil McKendrick, John Brewer and Roy Porter, *The Birth of a Consumer Society: The Commercialization of Eighteenth-Century England* (London: Europa Publications, 1982), 97.

13 Ibid., 40.

14 Fine and Leopold, *The World of Consumption*, 120 and 136.

15 Derek Hudson, *Munby Man of Two Worlds: The Life and Diaries of Arthur J. Munby, 1828–1910* (London: Abacus Books, 1974), 107.

16 Crane, *Fashion and Its Social Agendas*, 62.

17 Rachel Worth, *Fashion for the People: A History of Clothing at Marks & Spencer* (Oxford: Berg, 2007), 5.

18 Beverly Lemire, *Fashion's Favourite: The Cotton Trade and the Consumer in Britain, 1660–1800* (Oxford: Pasold Research Fund/Oxford University Press, 1991), 161.

19 Edwina Ehrman (ed.), *Fashioned from Nature* (London: V&A Publishing, 2018), 69.

20 Hamish Fraser, *The Coming of the Mass Market, 1850–1914* (London: Macmillan, 1981), 59.

21 Melanie Tebbutt, *Making Ends Meet: Pawnbroking and Working-Class Credit* (Leicester: Leicester University Press, 1983).

22 Lemire, *Fashion's Favourite*, 179.

23 Ibid., 199 and 200.

24 Ibid., 145. Lemire cites the draper's ledger of John and Mary Morgan of Neath, South Wales, which evidences orders of several sorts of ready-made gowns in the 1790s, for example, for the 'Super Chintz Gown' and the 'plain cotton gown'. In fact, Lemire says that the first orders for ready-made gowns associated with the cotton industry date to 1767 (187–8). She also gives the prices from an unidentified Manchester firm in 1778: the cheapest cotton gown cost 7s. 6d., just slightly more than the 6s. 6d. deemed by Sir Frederic Eden an acceptable expenditure for a common stuff gown (188).

25 Ellen Leopold, 'The Manufacture of the Fashion System', in *Chic Thrills: A Fashion Reader*, edited by J. Ash and E. Wilson (London: Pandora, 1992), 103.

26 Ibid., 113.

27 Ibid., 104.

28 C. Kidwell and M. Christman, *Suiting Everyone: The Democratization of Clothing in America* (Washington DC: Smithsonian Institute Press, published for the National Museum of History and Technology, 1974), 27.

29 Elizabeth Wilson and Lou Taylor, *Through the Looking Glass: A History of Dress from 1860 to the Present Day* (London: BBC Books, 1989), 33.

30 Jane Rendall, *Women in an Industrialising Society: England, 1750–1880* (Oxford: Basil Blackwell, 1990), 29.

31 Katrina Honeyman, *Well-Suited: A History of the Leeds Clothing Industry, 1850–1990* (Oxford: Oxford University Press, 2000), 22.

32 Arnold Bennett, *The Old Wives' Tale* (1908; this edn, Harmondsworth: Penguin, 1990), Book 4, ch. 5, III, 602–3.

33 Edward Shorter, *The History of Women's Bodies* (London: Allen Lane, 1983), 28.

34 Alison Adburgham, *Shops and Shopping, 1800–1914* (London: Barrie and Jenkins, 1981), 123.

35 Wilson and Taylor, *Through the Looking* Glass, 36.

36 Breward, Ehrman and Evans, *The London Look*, 37.

37 Lou Taylor, *Mourning Dress: A Costume and Social History* (London: George Allen and Unwin, 1983), 192–3.

38 Breward, Ehrman and Evans, *The London Look*, 32–3.

39 Pamela Sharpe, '"Cheapness and Economy": Manufacturing and Retailing Ready-Made Clothing in London and Essex 1830–50', *Textile History* 26:2 (1995): 203–13.

40 Alison Beazley, 'The Heavy and Light Clothing Industries 1850–1920', *Costume* 7 (1973): 55.

41 Kidwell and Christman, *Suiting Everyone*, 75.

42 Adburgham, *Shops and Shopping*, 128.

43 Fraser, *The Coming of the Mass Market*, 177.

44 Leopold, 'The Manufacture of the Fashion System', 104–5.

45 Ibid., 108.

46 Ibid., 172–3.

47 Angela John (ed.), *Unequal Opportunities: Women's Employment in England, 1800–1918* (Oxford: Basil Blackwell, 1985), 37.

48 Diary entry for *Thursday 2 June, 1859*, cited in Hudson, *Munby Man of Two Worlds*, 35.

49 Diary entry for *Friday 23 November, 1860*, cited in ibid., 83.

50 Diary entry for *Thursday 20 December, 1860*, cited in ibid., 86; emphases in the original.

51 Diary entry for *Tuesday 11 June, 1861*, cited in ibid., 99.

52 Diary entry for *Sunday, 20 July, 1861*, cited in ibid., 132.

53 Diary entry for *Friday 24 October, 1862*, cited in ibid., 138.

54 Diary entry for *Wednesday 1 June, 1864*, cited in ibid., 194.

55 Diary entry for *Saturday, 26 June, 1869*, cited in ibid., 272.

56 Diary entry for *Friday, 17 January, 1873*, cited in ibid., 319.

57 Honeyman, *Well-Suited*, 2.

58 Eric Sigsworth, *Montague Burton: The Tailor of Taste* (Manchester: Manchester University Press, 1990), 14.

59 Honeyman, *Well-Suited*, 53.

60 Ibid.

61 Ibid., 59.

62 Ibid., 65.

63 Ibid., 81.

64 Frank Mort, 'Paths to Mass Consumption: Britain and the USA since 1945', in *Buy This Book: Studies in Advertising and Consumption*, edited by Mica Nava et al. (London: Routledge, 1997), 19.

65 Ibid.

66 Fine and Leopold, *The World of Consumption*, 232.

6 Retailing revolution: Marks & Spencer and the democratisation of fashion

1 J. B. Jeffreys, *Retail Trading in Britain 1850–1959* (Cambridge: Cambridge University Press, 1954), 69–70.

2 Susannah Frankel, 'High Hopes', *Guardian Weekend* (7 February 1998), 38.

3 This chapter draws on research undertaken for my book, Rachel Worth, *Fashion for the People: A History of Clothing at Marks & Spencer* (Oxford: Berg, 2007).

4 Quoted in Asa Briggs, *Friends of the People: The Centenary History of Lewis's* (London: Batsford, 1956), 29.

5 Goronwy Rees, *A History of Marks & Spencer* (London: Weidenfeld and Nicolson, 1973), 9.

6 Ibid., 71.

7 Paul Bookbinder, *Simon Marks: Retail Revolutionary* (London: Weidenfeld and Nicolson, 1993), 90.

8 Israel Sieff, *The Memoirs of Israel Sieff* (London: Weidenfeld and Nicolson, 1970), 144.

9 Marcus Sieff, *Don't Ask the Price: The Memoirs of the President of Marks & Spencer* (London: Fontana, 1988), 60–1.

10 Sieff, *The Memoirs of Israel Sieff*, 145.

11 Harry Sacher, unpublished history *ca.* 1940s (Marks & Spencer Company Archive, University of Leeds), IV, 13.

12 Frank Mort, 'Paths to Mass Consumption: Britain and the USA since 1945', in *Buy This Book: Studies in Advertising and Consumption*, edited by Mica Nava et al. (London: Routledge, 1997), 18.

13 Eric Sigsworth, *Montague Burton: The Tailor of Taste* (Manchester: Manchester University Press, 1990), 54.

14 Christopher Breward, Edwina Ehrman and Caroline Evans, *The London Look: Fashion from Street to Catwalk* (New Haven: Yale University Press and the Museum of London, 2004), 90.

15 Hamish Fraser, *The Coming of the Mass Market, 1850–1914* (London: Macmillan, 1981), 58.

16 Ibid., 132.

17 Elizabeth Wilson and Lou Taylor, *Through the Looking Glass: A History of Dress from 1860 to the Present Day* (London: BBC Books, 1989), 77.

18 Breward, Ehrman and Evans, *The London Look*, 87.

19 G. Bowles and S. Kirrane, *Knitting Together: Memories of Leicestershire's Clothing Industry* (Leicester: Leicestershire Museums, Arts and Records Service, 1990), 36.

20 *Marks & Spencer Magazine* (1932), Marks & Spencer Company Archive, University of Leeds.

21 Quoted in Asa Briggs, *Marks and Spencer, 1884–1994: A Centenary History* (London: Octopus Books, 1984), 45.

22 At Marks & Spencer, no clothing in the period 1924–39 cost more than 5 shillings. In 1922 C&A was advertising a 'serviceable serge coat' at 15s. 11d.

(*Daily Chronicle*, 25 September 1922). This was more than three times the highest Marks & Spencer price point.

23 *Evening News*, 4 December 1922.

24 *Daily Mail*, 21 August 1922.

25 Lou Taylor, *The Study of Dress History* (Manchester: Manchester University Press, 2002), 52–3.

26 Wilson and Taylor, *Through the Looking Glass*, 95.

27 Rees, *A History of Marks & Spencer*, 96.

28 Bookbinder, *Simon Marks*, 101.

29 Sieff, *The Memoirs of Israel Sieff*, 156.

30 Rachel Worth, 'Fashioning the Clothing Product: Technology and Design at Marks & Spencer', *Textile History* 30:3 (1999): 234–50.

31 Wilson and Taylor, *Through the Looking Glass*, 116.

32 James Laver, *Concise History of Fashion* (London: Thames and Hudson, 1974), 252.

33 Wilson and Taylor, *Through the Looking Glass*, 120.

34 Elizabeth Ewing, *History of Twentieth-Century Fashion* (London: Batsford, 1993), 139–54.

35 Wilson and Taylor, *Through the Looking Glass*, 125.

36 Ibid., 110–11.

37 Ibid., 113.

38 Briggs, *Marks and Spencer, 1884–1994*, 55.

39 Rees, *A History of Marks & Spencer*, 162.

40 Marks & Spencer textile technologist Harry Atkinson worked with Harold Wilson at the Board of Trade to determine standards for Utility clothing, as well as advise on the correct allocation of clothes rationing coupons (Paul Bookbinder, *Marks & Spencer: The War Years, 1939–1945* (London: Century Benham, 1989), 45).

41 Ibid., 114.

42 *Textile Bulletin* No. 1, 27 February 1945, Marks & Spencer Company Archive, University of Leeds.

43 Letter from I. Glasman to B. Williams, 18 September 1981, Marks & Spencer Company Archive, University of Leeds.

44 *Drapers Record*, 1 March 1997: 7.

45 L. Goode, 'Cotton and Man-Made Fibres: A Retailer's View'. Paper for the Symposium on Inter-Fibre Competition, in conjunction with the 24th Plenary Meeting of the International Cotton Advisory Committee, May 1965, Marks & Spencer Company Archive, University of Leeds.

46 Ismar Glasman, 'Why Polyester? The Fibre of the '70s'. Paper for the Textile Technology Symposium, November 1969, Marks & Spencer Company Archive, University of Leeds.

47 Susannah Handley, *Nylon: The Manmade Fashion Revolution* (London: Bloomsbury Publishing, 1999), 50.

48 *St Michael News*, February 1972: 5.

49 Handley, *Nylon*, 72.

50 *St Michael News*, November 1960: 4.

51 Handley, *Nylon*, 70.

52 Ibid., 55.

53 Ibid., 114.

54 Ibid., 68.

55 Goode, 'Cotton and Man-Made Fibres: A Retailer's View'.

56 Anon., 'Analysis of Sales by Fibre', 2 February 1971, Marks & Spencer Company Archive, University of Leeds.

57 *St Michael News*, December 1958: 1.

58 Ibid., 4.

59 Elizabeth Roberts, *Women and Families: An Oral History, 1940–1970* (Oxford: Blackwell, 1995), 29.

60 Ibid., 33.

61 Ibid., 30.

62 *St Michael News*, September 1958: 4.

63 *St Michael News*, November 1972: 1.

64 *St Michael News*, May 1987: 5.

65 *St Michael News*, autumn 1961: 2.

66 *St Michael News*, December 1967: 6.

67 Ewing, *History of Twentieth Century Fashion*, 130.

68 *St Michael News*, February 1957: 1.

69 *St Michael News*, September 1990: 3.

70 *Draper's Record*, 10 August 1996: 5.

71 Philip Larkin, *The Large, Cool Store* (1961), stanzas 1–3.

72 Jennifer Craik, *The Face of Fashion: Cultural Studies in Fashion* (London: Routledge, 1993), 167.

7 Design and class

1 Jennifer Craik, *The Face of Fashion: Cultural Studies in Fashion* (London: Routledge, 1993), 167.

2 Emma McClendon, *Denim: Fashion's Frontier* (Newhaven: Yale University Press, 2016), 26.

3 Ibid., 27.

4 Craik, *The Face of Fashion*, 194–5.

5 McClendon, *Denim*, 11.

6 Ted Polhemus, *Street Style: From Sidewalk to Catwalk* (London: Thames and Hudson, 1994), 24.

7 Elizabeth Ewing, *History of Twentieth-Century Fashion* (London: Batsford, 1993), 157.

8 Ibid., see chapter 8.

9 Richard Lachlan worked as a designer for M&S for twenty years (1968–88), having trained at the Royal College of Art and worked for the designer Victor Stiebel. Richard provided this information to me in an interview (10 May 1996).

10 *St Michael News*, January 1967: 2.

11 Amy de la Haye (ed.), *The Cutting Edge – Fifty Years of British Fashion, 1947–1997* (London: V&A Publications, 1996), 206.

12 *The M&S Magazine*, spring 1988: 78.

13 Rachel Worth, *Fashion for the People: A History of Clothing at Marks & Spencer* (Oxford: Berg, 2007), 73–4.

14 *The M&S Magazine*, winter 1990: 60–1.

15 Roger Tredre, 'Shaping Up for the Hard Sell on the Soft Suit', *Independent* (22 September 1990): 32.

16 *The M&S Magazine*, summer 1995: 44–5.

17 Tamsin Blanchard, 'Off the Catwalk and on to the High Street', *Independent* (24 September 1996): 14.

18 Harriet Lane, 'Once Upon a Time, *fashion* and *Fashion* Were Very Different', *Observer* (30 November 1997): 27.

19 Ibid., 28.

20 Roger Tredre, 'Taking the Hauteur out of Couture', *Observer* (23 February 1997): 16.

21 Lisa Grainger, 'Nineties Look without a Label', *Times* (8 November 1997): 5.

22 Mimi Spencer, 'The Gospel According to *St Michael*', *Vogue* (April 1995), see whole article: 26–30.

23 Sally Brampton, 'The Adoration of St Michael', *Guardian* (8 October 1994), see whole article: 40–4 and 56.

24 Harriet Quick, 'Streets Ahead', *Guardian* (4 March 1995): 38.

25 A. A. Gill, 'The Way We Wear', *Times Style* (26 February 1995): 6.

26 Arthur House, 'Thirty Years Ago, Britain Gave the World Rave Culture', *Spectator* (12 August 2017). https://www.spectator.co.uk/2017/08/thirty-years-ago-britain-invented-acid-house/.

27 Marion Hume, 'And Soon to Be Seen in Your Local High Street', *Independent* (1 July 1993): 25; emphasis in the original.

28 Marion Hume, 'Punk Already?', *Independent* (24 June 1993): 17.

29 Marion Hume, 'The New Mood', *Independent on Sunday* (16 May 1993): 44.

30 *Guardian*, 25 March 1993 (front cover).

31 Roger Tredre, 'See What Crawled Up from Underground', *Independent* (10 December 1992): 17.

32 Ibid.

33 Ibid.

34 Ibid.

35 Suzanne Moore, 'Follies of Fashion', *Guardian* (22 January 1993): 11.

36 Ibid.

37 Brenda Pollen, 'Jagged Edge', *Elle* (May 1992): 112.

38 Susannah Frankel, 'A Magical Mystic', *Independent* (28 September 1996): 3.

39 Debbie Buckett, 'Raw Talent', *Guardian* (29 October 1992): 14.

40 Ibid.

41 Marion Hume, 'Coming Unstitched, or Just a Stitch-Up?', *Independent* (30 September 1993): 25.

42 Harriet Quick, 'Style File', *Guardian* (25 August 1994): 7.

43 Buckett, 'Raw Talent', 14.

44 Ibid. According to Buckett, Margiela is sometimes 'misrepresented' as 'a designer in deconstruction'.

45 Roger Tredre, 'From Belgium but Far from Boring', *Independent* (2 July 1992): 19.

46 Susannah Frankel, 'Rock Me, Baby', *Guardian* (3 May 1997): 38.

Conclusion

1 Teri Agins, *The End of Fashion: The Mass Marketing of the Clothing Business* (New York: William Morrow and Company, 1999), 16.

2 Ibid., 6.

3 Ibid., 8–11. Agins discusses the success of Gap, along with its sister divisions, Banana Republic and Old Navy, in more detail later in the book: together they gained an incredible market share in the 1990s and became the world's second apparel brand, behind Levi's. In 1998 – the year in which it opened a new store every day – Gap generated $8.3 billion in sales in its 2,237 stores, which included 953 Gap Stores, 637 Gap Kids stores, 258 Banana Republic stores and 282 Old Navy stores in the United States with the remaining Gap stores in Japan, the United Kingdom, Canada, France and German. The result was that people were now defining Gap and Banana Republic as fashion, even though these stores were charging $30 for a dress (185).

4 *Financial Times*, 26 July 2016: 44. Armstrong, however, also noted that after Johnson's change of role, he smartened himself up!

5 Agins, *The End of Fashion*, 152.

6   Ibid., 276.

7   Cited by Dilys Williams in *Fashioned from Nature*, edited by Edwina Ehrman
    (London: V&A Publishing, 2018), 157.

8   Ibid., 165.

9   Andrew Brooks, *Clothing Poverty: The Hidden World of Fast Fashion and
    Second-Hand Clothes* (London: Zed Books, 2015), 27.

10 https://www.greenpeace.org/international/story/6956/what-are-microfibers-and-
    why-are-our-clothes-polluting-the-oceans/ (accessed 16 November 2018).

11 Ehrman, *Fashioned from Nature*, 14.

12 Cited by Dilys Williams in *Fashioned from Nature*, 155. This book, which
    accompanied the V&A exhibition (21 April 2018 to 27 January 2019), focuses
    on the environmental impacts of fashion at a time when, as Emma Watson
    writes in the foreword, 'fashion is the second most polluting industry and
    fast fashion is the norm' (6). Kate Fletcher points out that 'it is estimated that
    clothing represents 5% to 10% of environmental impacts generated across the 25
    nations of the European Union … it is thought that 25% of chemicals produced
    worldwide are used for textiles and 20% of global industrial water pollution
    comes from textile dyeing and finishing' (*The Craft of Use: Post-Growth Fashion*
    (London: Routledge, 2016), 21).

13 Matilda Lee, *Eco-Chic: The Savvy Shopper's Guide to Ethical Fashion*
    (London: Octopus Books, 2007), back cover.

14 Marie Claire, June 2008: 13.

15 https://global.marksandspencer.com/plan-a/ (accessed 1 October 2018).

16 Fletcher, *The Craft of Use*, 21.

17 Ehrman, *Fashioned from Nature*, 27.

18 Helen Storey, quoted in Helen Storey, *Ten Years*, promotional material to
    celebrate ten years since launch of own label, edited by Sally Brampton (1994).

19 Brooks, *Clothing Poverty*, 32.

20 http://www.edelkoort.com/2015/09/anti_fashion-manifesto/ (Trend Union, Paris,
    2014; second edn 2015) (accessed 26 September 2018).

21 Ibid.

22 Ibid.

23 Ibid.

24 Brooks, *Clothing Poverty*, 216.

25 Fletcher, *The Craft of Use*, 17.

Bibliography

Adburgham, Alison. *Shops and Shopping, 1800–1914*. London: Barrie and
 Jenkins, 1981.

Agins, Teri. *The End of Fashion: The Mass Marketing of the Clothing Business*.
 New York: William Morrow and Company, 1999.

Allestree, Richard. *The Whole Duty of Man*. London, 1671.

Arch, Joseph. *Joseph Arch: The Story of His Life Told by Himself*. 1898; this edn,
 London: MacGibbon & Kee, 1966.

Arnold, Rebecca. *Fashion: A Very Short Introduction*. Oxford: Oxford University
 Press, 2009.

Austen, Jane. *Sense and Sensibility*. 1811; this edn, London: Penguin Classic Random
 House, 2014.

Balzac, Honoré de. *Old Goriot*. 1835; this edn translated with an introduction by A. J.
 Krailsheimer. Oxford: Oxford World's Classics, Oxford University Press, 2009.

Beazley, Alison. 'The Heavy and Light Clothing Industries 1850–1920'. *Costume* 7
 (1973): 55–9.

Bennett, Arnold. *The Old Wives' Tale*. 1908; this edn, Harmondsworth:
 Penguin, 1990.

Bookbinder, Paul. *Marks & Spencer: The War Years, 1939–1945*. London: Century
 Benham, 1989.

Bookbinder, Paul. *Simon Marks: Retail Revolutionary*. London: Weidenfeld and
 Nicolson, 1993.

Bourdieu, Pierre. *Distinction: A Social Critique of the Judgment of Taste*. First
 published in France in 1979; this edn translated by Richard Nice. London:
 Routledge and Kegan Paul, 1984.

Bowles, G. and Kirrane, S. *Knitting Together: Memories of the Leicestershire Clothing
 Industry*. Leicester: Leicestershire Museums, Arts and Records Service, 1990.

Braudel, Ferdinand. *Civilisation and Capitalism, 15th to 18th Century*. 3 vols. Vol.
 I: *The Structures of Everyday Life*. London, 1981.

Breward, Christopher. *The Culture of Fashion*. Manchester: Manchester University
 Press, 1995.

Breward, Christopher. *Fashioning London: Clothing and the Modern Metropolis*.
 Oxford: Berg, 2004.

Breward, Christopher, Ehrman, Edwina and Evans, Caroline. *The London Look: Fashion from Street to Catwalk*. New Haven: Yale University Press and the Museum of London, 2004.

Briggs, Asa. *Friends of the People: The Centenary History of Lewis's*. London: Batsford, 1956.

Briggs, Asa. *Marks and Spencer, 1884–1994: A Centenary History*. London: Octopus Books, 1984.

Brooks, Andrew. *Clothing Poverty: The Hidden World of Fast Fashion and Second-Hand Clothes*. London: Zed Books, 2015.

Brun, M. Le. *Le Journal de la Mode et du Goût*. Various 'cahiers' from 25 February 1790 to 20 November 1792.

Bullen, Elizabeth. 'Class'. In *Keywords for English Literature*. Edited by Philip Nel and Lissa Paul, 48. New York: New York University Press, 2011.

Burney, Fanny, *Evelina*. 1778; this edn, Oxford: Oxford University Press, 1987.

Byrde, Penelope. *Jane Austen Fashion: Fashion and Needlework in the Works of Jane Austen*. Ludlow: Excellent Press, 1999.

Calhoun, Craig. *The Question of Class Struggle: Social Foundations of Popular Radicalism during the Industrial Revolution*. Oxford: Basil Blackwell, 1982.

Chapple, J. A. V. and Pollard, A. *The Letters of Mrs Gaskell*. Manchester: Manchester University Press, 1966.

Chrisman-Campbell, Kimberley. 'From Baroque Elegance to the French Revolution 1700–1790'. In *The Fashion Reader*. Edited by Linda Welters and Abby Lillethun, 6–19. Oxford: Berg, 2007.

Cobbett, William. *Rural Rides*. 1830; this edn with an Introduction by George Woodcock. Harmondsworth: Penguin, 1987.

Collins, Wilkie. *No Name*. Published in serial form during 1862–3; in 3 vols, December 1862, by Sampson Low, Son and Co; this edn, Oxford: Oxford University Press, 1986.

Craik, Jennifer. *The Face of Fashion: Cultural Studies in Fashion*. London: Routledge, 1993.

Crane, Diana. *Fashion and Its Social Agendas: Class, Gender, and Identity in Clothing*. Chicago: University of Chicago Press, 2000.

Curry, Patrick. 'Towards a Post-Marxist Social History: Thompson, Clark and Beyond'. In *Rethinking Social History: English Society 1570–1920 and Its Interpretation*. Edited by Adrian Wilson, 158–200. Manchester: Manchester University Press, 1993.

Davidson, Peter. *The Last of the Light: About Twilight*. London: Reaktion, 2015.

Dickens, Charles. *A Tale of Two Cities*. 1859; this edn, Harmondsworth: Penguin, 1980.

Dyck, Ian. 'Towards the "Cottage Charter": The Expressive Culture of Farm Workers in Nineteenth-Century England'. *Rural History* 1:1 (1990): 95–112.

Ehrman, Edwina (ed.). *Fashioned from Nature*. London: V&A Publishing, 2018.

Eliot, George. *Adam Bede*. First published in serial form in Blackwood's Magazine, from February 1859. Harmondsworth: Penguin Popular Classics, 1994.

Eliot, George. *The Mill on the Floss*. First published in 3 vols by William Blackwood and Sons. Edinburgh: William Blackwood and Sons, 1860.

Eliot, George. *Felix Holt, the Radical*. First published in 3 vols by William Blackwood and Sons. Edinburgh: William Blackwood and Sons, 1866.

Encyclopedia of Textiles. Edited by the American Fabrics Magazine. Doric Publishing Co, 1960.

Engels, Friedrich. *The Condition of the Working Class in England in 1844*. First authorised English translation published in New York in 1887 and in London in 1892; this edn with an Introduction by Eric Hobsbawm. Granada Publishing, 1969.

Ewing, Elizabeth. *Fur in Dress*. London: Batsford, 1981.

Ewing, Elizabeth. *History of Twentieth-Century Fashion*. London: Batsford, 1993.

Fine, Ben and Leopold, Ellen. *The World of Consumption*. London: Routledge, 1993.

Fletcher, Kate. *The Craft of Use: Post-Growth Fashion*. London: Routledge, 2016.

Fraser, Hamish. *The Coming of the Mass Market, 1850–1914*. London: Macmillan, 1981.

Gaskell, Elizabeth. *The Letters of Mrs Gaskell*. Edited by J. A. V. Chapple and A. Pollard. Manchester: Manchester University Press, 1966.

Gaskell, Elizabeth. *Mary Barton*. First published anonymously in 1848 in 2 vols by Chapman and Hall; this edn with an Introduction by Stephen Gill. Harmondsworth: Penguin Classics, 1970.

Gaskell, Elizabeth. *North and South*. First published in Charles Dickens's *Household Words* in 22 weekly instalments, September 1854 to January 1855; first published in novel form in 1855; this edn, Harmondsworth: Penguin Popular Classics, 1994.

Handley, Susannah. *Nylon: The Manmade Fashion Revolution*. London: Bloomsbury Publishing, 1999.

Hardy, Thomas. 'The Dorsetshire Labourer'. *Longman's Magazine*, vol. 2 (1883): 252–69.

Haye, Amy de la (ed.). *The Cutting Edge – Fifty Years of British Fashion, 1947–1997*. London: V&A Publications, 1996.

Hobsbawm, E. J. and Rudé, George. *Captain Swing*. 1969; this edn, Harmondsworth: Penguin, 1985.

Howkins, Alun. 'Labour History and the Rural Poor 1850–1980'. *Rural History* 1:1 (1990): 113–22.

Hudson, Derek. *Munby Man of Two Worlds: The Life and Diaries of Arthur J. Munby, 1828–1910*. London: Abacus Books, 1974.

Huxley, Aldous. *Brave New World*. 1932; this edn, London: Flamingo, 1994.

Jefferies, Richard. 'Wiltshire Labourers'. *The Times*, 12 November 1872; published here in *Landscape with Figures: An Anthology of Richard Jefferies' Prose*. Harmondsworth: Penguin, 1983.

Jeffreys, J. B. *Retail Trading in Britain, 1850–1959*. Cambridge: Cambridge University Press, 1954.

John, Angela (ed.). *Unequal Opportunities: Women's Employment in England, 1800–1918*. Oxford: Basil Blackwell, 1985.

Joyce, Patrick. *Visions of the People: Industrial England and the Question of Class, 1840–1914*. Cambridge: Cambridge University Press, 1991.

Joyce, Patrick. *Class*. Oxford: Oxford University Press, 1995.

Keating, Peter. *The Haunted Study: A Social History of the English Novel, 1875–1914*. London: Fontana Press, 1991.

Kidwell, C. and Christman, M. *Suiting Everyone: The Democratization of Clothing in America*. Washington DC: Smithsonian Institute Press, published for the National Museum of History and Technology, 1974.

Kingsley, Charles. *Yeast*. Published in Fraser's Magazine in 1848 and in book form in 1851; this edn, London: Macmillan, 1895.

Larkin, Philip. *The Large, Cool Store*. First published in *Times Literary Supplement*, 14 July 1961; then in *The Whitsun Weddings*. This edition of *Collected Poems* edited by Anthony Thwaite. London: Faber and Faber, 2003.

Laski, Marghanita. *George Eliot and Her World*. London: Thames and Hudson, 1978.

Laslett, Peter. *The World We Have Lost*. 1965; this edn, Cambridge: Cambridge University Press, 1979.

Laver, James. *Concise History of Fashion*. London: Thames and Hudson, 1974.

Lawrence, D. H. *The Rainbow*. 1915; this edn, Harmondsworth: Penguin, 1981.

Lemire, Beverly. *Fashion's Favourite: The Cotton Trade and the Consumer in Britain, 1660–1800*. Oxford: Pasold Research Fund, 1991.

Leopold, Ellen. 'The Manufacture of the Fashion System'. In *Chic Thrills: A Fashion Reader*. Edited by Juliet Ash and Elizabeth Wilson, 101–17. London: Pandora, 1992.

Levitt, Sarah. *Fashion in Photographs, 1880–1900*. London: Batsford, 1991.

McClendon, Emma. *Denim: Fashion's Frontier*. New Haven: Yale University Press, 2016.

McKendrick, Neil, Brewer, John and Plumb, J. H. *The Birth of a Consumer Society: The Commercialisation of Eighteenth-Century England*. London: Europa Publications, 1982.

Mendes, Valerie. *Black in Fashion*. London: V&A Publications, 1999.

Mingay, G. E. *Rural Life in Victorian England*. Stroud: Alan Sutton Publishing, 1990.

Mort, Frank. *Cultures of Consumption, Masculinities and Social Space in Late Twentieth-Century Britain*. London: Routledge, 1996.

Mort, Frank. 'Paths to Mass Consumption: Britain and the USA since 1945'. In *Buy This Book: Studies in Advertising and Consumption*. Edited by Mica Nava et al. London: Routledge, 1997.

Neale, R. S. *Class and Ideology in the Nineteenth Century*. London: Routledge and Kegan Paul, 1972.

Newby, Howard. *Country Life: A Social History of Rural England*. London: Weidenfeld and Nicolson, 1987.

O'Keefe, Linda. *Shoes: A Celebration of Pumps, Sandals, Slippers and More*. New York: Workman Publishing, 1996.

Parliamentary Papers, *Second Report from the Commissioners on the Employment of Children, Young Persons and Women in Agriculture, with Appendix Part I and Part II 1868–9*. Facsimile published. Shannon: Irish University Press, 1968.

Pickering, Paul A. 'Class without Words: Symbolic Communication in the Chartist Movement'. *Past and Present* 112 (1986): 144–63.

Pointon, Marcia. *Portrayal and the Search for Identity*. London: Reaktion, 2013.

Polhemus, Ted. *Street Style: From Sidewalk to Catwalk*. London: Thames and Hudson, 1994; updated in 2010 by PYMCA (Photographic Youth Music Culture Archive).

Rees, Goronwy. *A History of Marks & Spencer*. London: Weidenfeld and Nicolson, 1973.

Rendall, Jane. *Women in an Industrialising Society: England, 1750–1880*. Oxford: Basil Blackwell, 1990.

Ribeiro, Aileen. *Fashion in the French Revolution*. London: Batsford, 1988.

Richmond, Vivienne (ed.). *Clothing, Society and Culture in Nineteenth-Century England*. Vol. 3, *Working-Class Dress*. London: Pickering & Chatto, 2013.

Riello, Giorgio. *Cotton: The Fabric That Made the Modern World*. Cambridge: Cambridge University Press, 2013.

Roberts, Elizabeth. *Women and Families: An Oral History, 1940–1970*. Oxford: Blackwell, 1995.

Robinson, Marilynne. *When I Was a Child I Read Books*. London: Virago, 2012.

Roche, Daniel. *The Culture of Clothing: Dress and Fashion in the Ancien Régime*. 1989; translated into English in 1994; this edn, Cambridge: Cambridge University Press, 1996.

Rousseau, Jean-Jacques. 'Considération sur les avantages de changer le costume français par la société populaire et républicaine des Arts'. *La Décade philosophique littéraire et politique*, 10 Floréal, Year III (1795): 60–2.

Rousseau, Jean-Jacques. *Reveries of the Solitary Walker.* 1792 (anonymously); this translation with an introduction by Peter France. Harmondsworth: Penguin, 1979.

Seymour-Jones, Carole. *Woman of Conflict.* London: Allison and Busby, 1992.

Sharpe, Pamela. '"Cheapness and Economy": Manufacturing and Retailing Ready-Made Clothing in London and Essex 1830–50'. *Textile History* 26:2 (1995): 203–13.

Shorter, Edward. *The History of Women's Bodies.* London: Allen Lane, 1983.

Sieff, Israel. *The Memoirs of Israel Sieff.* London: Weidenfeld and Nicolson, 1970.

Sieff, Marcus. *Don't Ask the Price: The Memoirs of the President of Marks & Spencer.* London: Fontana, 1988.

Sigsworth, Eric. *Montague Burton, The Tailor of Taste.* Manchester: Manchester University Press, 1990.

Simmel, Georg. 'Fashion'. *International Quarterly* 10:1 (October 1904): 130–55. (Reprinted in *American Journal of Sociology* 62:6 (May 1957): 541–58.)

Smith, Hubert Llewellyn (ed.). *The New Survey of London Life and Labour,* vol. 2. London: King & Son, 1930.

Somerville, Alexander. *The Whistler at the Plough – Containing Travels, Statistics and Descriptions of Scenery and Agricultural Customs in Most Parts of England.* 1852; this edn with an introduction by Keith D. M. Snell. London: Merlin Press, 1979.

Steele, Valerie, 'The Social and Political Significance of Macaroni Fashion'. *Costume* 19 (1985): 94–109.

Storey, Helen. *Ten Years.* Promotional material to celebrate ten years since launch of own label. Edited by Sally Brampton, 1994.

Styles, John. *The Dress of the People: Everyday Fashion in Eighteenth-Century England.* New Haven: Yale University Press, 2007.

Styles, John. *Threads of Feeling: The London Foundling Hospital's Textile Tokens, 1740–1770.* London: The Foundling Museum, 2010.

Tamboukou, Maria. *Sewing, Writing and Fighting: Radical Practices in Work, Politics and Culture.* London: Rowman and Littlefield, 2016.

Taylor, Lou. *Mourning Dress: A Costume and Social History.* London: George Allen and Unwin, 1983.

Taylor, Lou. *The Study of Dress History.* Manchester: Manchester University Press, 2002.

Tebbutt, Melanie. *Making Ends Meet: Pawnbroking and Working-Class Credit.* Leicester: Leicester University Press, 1983.

Thompson, E. P. *The Making of the English Working Class.* London: Pelican, 1963.

Todd, Selina. *The Rise and Fall of the Working Class, 1910–2010.* London: John Murray, 2014.

Tozer, Jane and Levitt, Sarah. *Fabric of Society: A Century of People and Their Clothes, 1770–1870*. Carno: Laura Ashley, 1983.

Trollope, Anthony. *The Warden*. 1855; this edn, London: J.M. Dent and Sons Ltd, 1907.

Uglow, Jenny. *A Habit of Stories*. London: Faber and Faber, 1993.

Veblen, Theodore. *The Theory of the Leisure Class: An Economic Study in the Evolution of Institutions*. New York: Macmillan, 1899.

Vincent, Susan. *Dressing the Elite: Clothes in Early Modern England*. Oxford: Berg, 2003.

Warwick, Alexandra and Cavallaro, Dani. *Fashioning the Frame: Boundaries, Dress and the Body*. Oxford: Berg, 1998.

Welters, Linda and Lillethun, Abby (eds). *The Fashion Reader*. Oxford: Berg, 2007.

Wilson, Elizabeth and Taylor, Lou. *Through the Looking Glass: A History of Dress from 1860 to the Present Day*. London: BBC Books, 1989.

Wiseman, Marjorie, 'Acquisition or Inheritance? Material Goods in Paintings by Vermeer and His Contemporaries'. In *Vermeer and the Masters of Genre Painting: Inspiration and Rivalry*. Edited by Adrian E. Waiboer, 51–63. New Haven: Yale University Press, 2017.

Woolf, Virginia. *The New Dress*. 1927; this edn published in Virginia Woolf's *A Haunted House and Other Stories*. New York: Mariner Books, 2002, 47–57.

Woolf, Virginia. *A Room of One's Own*. 1928; this edn, London: Penguin, 2004.

Worth, Rachel. 'Elizabeth Gaskell, Clothes and Class Identity'. *Costume* 32 (1998): 52–9.

Worth, Rachel. 'Fashioning the Clothing Product: Technology and Design at Marks & Spencer'. *Textile History* 30:3 (1999): 234–50.

Worth, Rachel. *Fashion for the People: A History of Clothing at Marks & Spencer*. Oxford: Berg, 2007.

Worth, Rachel. *Clothing and Landscape in Victorian England: Working-Class Dress and Rural Life*. London: I. B. Tauris, 2018.

Magazine and newspaper articles

Armstrong, Robert. *Financial Times*, 26 July 2016: 44.

Blanchard, Tamsin. 'Off the Catwalk and on to the High Street'. *Independent*, 24 September 1996: 14–15.

Brampton, Sally. 'The Adoration of St Michael'. *Guardian*, 8 October 1994: 40–4 and 56.

Buckett, Debbie. 'Raw Talent'. *Guardian*, 29 October 1992: 14–15.

Colls, Robert. 'The Making and the Man'. *Times Higher Education Supplement*, 21 November 2013: 42–5.

Dorling, Danny. 'Just Who Do You Think You Are?', *Times Higher Education Supplement*, 12 November 2015: 50.

Frankel, Susannah. 'A Magical Mystic'. *Independent*, 28 September 1996: 2–4.

Frankel, Susannah. 'Rock Me, Baby'. *Guardian*, 3 May 1997: 38–9.

Frankel, Susannah. 'High Hopes'. *Guardian Weekend*, 7 February 1998: 38–43.

Gill, A. A. 'The Way We Wear'. *Times Style*, 26 February 1995: 6.

Grainger, Lisa. 'Nineties Look without a Label'. *Times*, 8 November 1997: 5.

House, Arthur. 'Thirty Years Ago, Britain Gave the World Rave Culture'. *Spectator*, 12 August 2017. https://www.spectator.co.uk/2017/08/thirty-years-ago-britain-invented-acid-house/.

Hume, Marion. 'The New Mood'. *Independent on Sunday*, 16 May 1993: 44 and 48.

Hume, Marion. 'Punk Already?' *Independent*, 24 June 1993: 17.

Hume, Marion. 'And Soon to Be Seen in Your Local High Street'. *Independent*, 1 July 1993: 25.

Hume, Marion. 'Coming Unstitched, or Just a Stitch-Up?' *Independent*, 30 September 1993: 25.

Lane, Harriet. 'Once Upon a Time, *fashion* and *Fashion* Were Very Different'. *Observer*, 30 November 1997: 24–8.

Moore, Suzanne. 'Follies of Fashion'. *Guardian*, 22 January 1993: 11.

Moore, Suzanne. 'The Left Doesn't Understand Working-Class Tories'. *Guardian*, 14 May 2015: 5.

Pollen, Brenda. 'Jagged Edge'. *Elle*, May 1992: 112.

Quick, Harriet. 'Style Guide', *Guardian*, 25 August 1994: 7.

Quick, Harriet, 'Streets Ahead'. *Guardian*, 4 March 1995: (38–9) 38.

Spencer, Mimi. 'The Gospel According to *St Michael*'. *Vogue*, April 1995: 26–30.

Tredre, Roger. 'Shaping Up for the Hard Sell on the Soft Suit'. *Independent*, 22 September 1990: 32.

Tredre, Roger. 'From Belgium but Far from Boring'. *Independent*, 2 July 1992: 19.

Tredre, Roger. 'See What Crawled Up from Underground'. *Independent*, 10 December 1992: 17.

Tredre, Roger. 'Taking the Hauteur out of Couture'. *Observer*, 23 February 1997: 16.

Unpublished documents in the Marks & Spencer Company Archive, University of Leeds (listed chronologically)

Marks & Spencer Magazine, 1932.

Sacher, Harry. Unpublished history (*ca.* 1940s).

Textile Bulletin, no. 1, 27 February 1945.

St Michael News, February 1957: 1.

St Michael News, September 1958: 4.

St Michael News, December 1958:1.

St Michael News, November 1960: 4.

St Michael News, autumn 1961: 2.

Goode, L. 'Cotton and Man-Made Fibres: A Retailer's View'. Paper for the Symposium on Inter-Fibre Competition, in conjunction with the 24th Plenary Meeting of the International Cotton Advisory Committee, May 1965.

St Michael News, January 1967: 2.

St Michael News, December 1967: 6.

Glasman, I. 'Why Polyester? The Fibre of the '70s'. Paper for the Textile Technology Symposium, November 1969.

Anon., 'Analysis of Sales by Fibre'. 2 February 1971.

St Michael News, February 1972: 5.

St Michael News, November 1972: 1.

Letter from I. Glasman to B. Williams, 18 September 1981.

St Michael News, May 1987: 5.

The M&S Magazine, spring 1988: 78.

St Michael News, September 1990: 3.

The M&S Magazine, winter 1990: 60–1.

The M&S Magazine, summer 1995: 44–5.

Magazine and newspaper articles with no specific author

Daily Mail, 21 August 1922.

Daily Chronicle, 25 September 1922.

Guardian, 25 March 1993 (front cover).

Draper's Record, 10 August 1996: 5.

Draper's Record, 1 March 1997: 7

Evening News, 4 December 1922.
Marie Claire, June 2008 (entire issue).

Websites

http://www.edelkoort.com/2015/09/anti_fashion-manifesto/ (Trend Union, Paris, 2014; second edn 2015) (accessed 26 September 2018).
https://global.marksandspencer.com/plan-a/ (accessed 1 October 2018).
https://www.greenpeace.org/international/story/6956/what-are-microfibers-and-why-are-our-clothes-polluting-the-oceans/ (accessed 16 November 2018).

Index

Page numbers in *italics* refer to illustrations.